Green Engineering and Technology:
Concepts and Applications

Green Automation for
Sustainable Environment

Green Engineering and Technology: Concepts and Applications

Series Editors:
Brojo Kishore Mishra
GIET University, India

Raghvendra Kumar
LNCT College, India

Green Innovation, Sustainable Development, and Circular Economy
Edited by Himanshu Sharma, Siddhartha Pandey, Nitin Kumar Singh, and Sunkulp Goel

Green Automation for Sustainable Environment
Edited by Sherin Zafar, Mohd Abdul Ahad, M. Afshar Alam, and Kashish Ara Shakil

Green Automation for Sustainable Environment

Edited by
Sherin Zafar, Mohd Abdul Ahad,
M. Afshar Alam, and Kashish Ara Shakil

CRC Press
Taylor & Francis Group
Boca Raton London New York

CRC Press is an imprint of the
Taylor & Francis Group, an **informa** business

First edition published 2021
by CRC Press
6000 Broken Sound Parkway NW, Suite 300, Boca Raton, FL 33487-2742

and by CRC Press
2 Park Square, Milton Park, Abingdon, Oxon, OX14 4RN

© 2021 Taylor & Francis Group, LLC

CRC Press is an imprint of Taylor & Francis Group, LLC

ISBN: 978-0-367-42238-7 (hbk)
ISBN: 978-0-367-55125-4 (pbk)
ISBN: 978-1-003-00079-2 (ebk)

Typeset in Times
by codeMantra

Visit the companion website/eResources: www.routledge.com/9780367422387

Contents

Contents

Preface

With a changing environment and limited natural resources, there is a massive requirement of novel and technical solutions. Green computing is one such approach for changing the conventional methodologies adopted by traditional techniques to achieve conservation of energy and making our environment cleaner by utilizing renewable sources and resources of energy. This book invites original contributions, novel ideas, approaches, frameworks, and architectures which focus on making the environment sustainable through innovative engineering and green computing approaches. It will further explore concepts and the role of green computing and its recent developments for making the environment sustainable. It will also focus on green automation not limited to computers but also various disciplines such as nanoscience, information technology (IT), biochemistry, IoT, and sensors. This book is characterized through descriptions of sustainability, green computing, and their relevance to the environment and society as a whole.

The topics of interest includes, but not limited to, the following:

- Green computing and its related technologies
- Sustainable approaches for computing
- Energy-efficient computing
- Role of IoT and sensors in achieving sustainability
- Role of Big Data analytics in sustainability
- Novel and energy-efficient storage solutions
- Green cloud environment
- Edge/fog computing
- Sustainable smart spaces
- Green automation in data centers
- Wireless networks and related security protocols
- Energy-efficient data management and data transfer
- Sustainable Big Data architectures
- Security issues and challenges in green automation and sustainable computing
- Challenges and opportunities with green and sustainable computing in healthcare, agriculture, and society.

Editors

Dr. Sherin Zafar

Assistant Professor, Department of CSE, Jamia Hamdard, zafarsherin@gmail.com

Sherin Zafar is currently an Assistant Professor in the Department of Computer Science, School of Engineering Sciences & Technology, Jamia Hamdard, New Delhi, India, and a joint supervisor of PhD students Deepa Mehta (11/PHD/0016), working on "Optimization In ZRP Through Neoteric Routing Approach" in Manav Rachna University, Faridabad, India, and Neha Sharma (160020601005) and Ashu Gautam (160020601005), working on "Trust-Based Neoteric Optimized Routing Approach for MANET" in GD Goenka University, Sohna, India. She has 13+ years of teaching experience. She received her PhD from Manav Rachna International Institute of Research and Studies (MRIU) Faridabad on "Optimized Secure Protocol for MANET using Biometric Approach" with a CGPA of 8.36 under the guidance of Prof. M.K Soni, Former Professor, NIT Kurukshetra, India, and currently Pro. Vice Chancellor, MRIU; and Prof. M.M.S Beg, Principal of Zakir Hussain College of Engineering, Aligarh Muslim University, India. She published a patent on 31 May 2019: "System & Method Thereof for Secure Digital Health Network Based on Distributed Ledger Technology." She is a reviewer for 41 journals. She has reviewed around 80 papers and has published around 50 research papers and chapters in Scopus, SCI, and referred and impact factor journals and conferences.

Dr. Mohd Abdul Ahad

Assistant Professor, Department of CSE, Jamia Hamdard, itsmeahad@ieee.org

Mohd Abdul Ahad is currently an Assistant Professor in the Department of Computer Science and Engineering, School of Engineering Sciences and Technology, Jamia Hamdard, New Delhi, India. He has a rich experience of more than 11 years in the field of computer science and engineering. He obtained his PhD degree in the field of Big Data architecture. His research areas include Big Data architecture, distributed computing, IoT, and sustainable computing. He has published several research papers in various international journals of repute. He has chaired several sessions in international conferences of Springer, Elsevier, etc. He is a certified Microsoft Innovative Educator and a certified Google Educator. He is a life member of Indian Society of Technical Education (ISTE) as well as an active member of IEEE and ACM.

Prof. M. Afshar Alam

Professor, Department of CSE, Jamia Hamdard, aalam@jamiahamdard.ac.in

M. Afshar Alam is a Professor, Dean, and Head of the Department of Computer Science and Engineering, School of Engineering Sciences and Technology, Jamia Hamdard, New Delhi, India. He has a rich teaching and research experience of more than 24 years. He has guided more than 25 PhD students. He has published more than 130 research papers in various international journals and conferences of repute. He is also a member of several high power committee of Government of India agencies such as Department of Science & Technology (DST), University Grants Commission (UGC), Science and Engineering Research Board (SERB), and Ministry of Human Resource Development (MHRD).

Dr. Kashish Ara Shakil

Assistant Professor, Princess Nourah Bint Abdul, Rahman University,
shakilkashish@yahoo.com

Kashish Ara Shakil is an Assistant Professor in the Department of Computer Science, Princess Nourah Bint Abdul Rahman University, Riyadh, Saudi Arabia. She is a great researcher and published about 40 papers in Scopus and referred and indexed journals and conferences. She has Google Scholar citations of 218, h-index of 10, and i-10 index of 10. Her highest impact factor is 3.44. She has 5 years of experience in academic research institute and more than one year of experience in IT with specialties in cloud computing and handling Big Data. She has delivered live lectures for University Grants Commission- Consortium for Educational Communication (Government of India). She has been a visiting researcher (honorary Appointment) in University of Melbourne, Australia, and has worked on the development of AI-based scheduling algorithms for resource allocation on scientific workflows in cloud. She received her PhD in cloud computing from Jamia Millia Islamia, New Delhi, India, with the doctoral thesis topic "An Effective Framework for Data Management in a Cloud-Based System."

Contributors

Ranjit Biswas
Jamia Hamdard, New Delhi, India

Shikha Brahmachari
Netaji Subhas University of Technology,
New Delhi, India

Zeeshan A. Haq
Jamia Hamdard, New Delhi, India

Imran Hussain
Jamia Hamdard, New Delhi, India

Aqeel Khalique
Jamia Hamdard, New Delhi, India

Tabrej A. Khan
Jamia Hamdard, New Delhi, India

Insha Naz
Jamia Hamdard, New Delhi, India

Sameena Naaz
Jamia Hamdard, New Delhi, India

Anam Saiyeda
Jamia Hamdard, New Delhi, India

Deepak Kumar Sharma
Netaji Subhas University of Technology,
New Delhi, India

Ishaan Srivastav
Netaji Subhas University of Technology,
New Delhi, India

Safdar Tanweer
Jamia Hamdard, New Delhi, India

Amita Yadav
MSIT, New Delhi, India

1 Green Computing in Wireless Sensor Networks through Energy-Efficient Techniques for Lifetime Improvement

Amita Yadav
MSIT

CONTENTS

1.1 INTRODUCTION

The technological advancement in wireless communication has led to the development of wireless sensor networks (WSNs). With the exceptional capability of not only sensing but processing, WSNs became popular and very much required for many applications. Sensor nodes are small and are deployed in the monitoring area in large amount to detect events. But they are resource constrained. They are tiny nodes with low-cost processor, limited storage capacity, limited transceiver range

1

and limited battery lifetime. Sensor nodes sense the monitoring area such as forests, fields, underwater areas, cities, human body, etc. and transmit the sensed data to the sink. This transmission may take place via single hop or through multi-hops. In single-hop networks, nodes can directly send data to the sink. But generally, a sensor network field is large and the node transmission range is limited, so the nodes may send data to the sink via intermediate nodes or forwarding nodes, which is called as the multi-hop network [1]. In single hop, sensor nodes deplete their energy due to direct data transmission, whereas in a multi-hop, the forwarding nodes deplete their energy and reduce the network lifetime. The lifetime of sensor nodes mainly depends upon a finite source of energy like battery. Therefore, it is crucial to consider the energy-efficient techniques to increase the life span of the network and consequently their role in green computing.

1.2 TAXONOMY OF ENERGY-EFFICIENT ROUTING PROTOCOLS

There are a few common requirements of sensor networks for all types of applications in WSN, which are given as follows [2]:

1. *Network lifetime* – Nodes are deployed in an unattended environment; therefore, it is required to conserve energy of nodes and prolong the network lifetime. If a network fails due to energy depletion of nodes, communication failure occurs.
2. *Network size* – Sensor nodes are deployed in a large network area to detect more events. A large coverage area is the interest of most applications.
3. *Minimum faults* – Data packet may be lost in transmission of data to the sink. Many events may be missed, and monitoring of environment is broken. Data reliability is the major concern of applications.

The sensor nodes are generally deployed in an inaccessible area. These sensor nodes are limited in battery power, and replacement of batteries is not an easy task in remote areas. The major challenge is to keep the network alive. A limited battery power makes it difficult to manage and monitor the network. Therefore, it is required to conserve the node energy in order to increase the network life span.

Various sources of energy dissipation, which we have already discussed in the previous chapter, are idle listening, collisions, over-hearing, over-emitting, etc.

1.2.1 ENERGY CONSERVATION TECHNIQUES

Various ways for conserving energy are discussed in Ref. [3], which are given as follows:

1. Sensor nodes consume equal amount of energy in ready mode as well as in receiving mode; therefore, sleep mode and a wake-up schedule must be set for event sensing to save energy. The idle scheduling time depends on the network traffic.

2. To conserve the energy in WSNs, the sensor network nodes use data fusion. Using data fusion, the amount of data transmitted from sensor nodes to the base station is reduced. Data fusion combines one or more data packets from different sensor nodes to produce a single packet. Also, data must be aggregated to reduce the transmission load. Sensor network is divided into clusters. Member nodes in the cluster send the data to the cluster head (CH), where the data is aggregated and data fusion takes place.
3. In WSN, data processing is much cheaper than data transmission. Data compression performed through various algorithms saves energy.
4. In a clustered network, CHs aggregate the data and transmit it to the base station (BS). The responsibility of a CH node is more as compared to the member nodes in the network. Therefore, CH consumes more energy or dies quickly in a homogeneous network. The communication load must be balanced to increase the lifetime of the network. Load balancing technique equally distributes the traffic load in the network, and a good network performance can be attained. Load balancing of CHs can be achieved through a random rotation of CH. It can also be achieved via appointing advanced nodes as CH in a heterogeneous network as they have more battery power.
5. By lowering the transmission range, the energy can be conserved, but network coverage is still required. Therefore, a mechanism that takes care of transmission range as well as coverage of network is needed. Heterogeneous sensor networks consider the concept of remaining energy and distance [4].

There are different layers which work in their own way to achieve energy efficiency.

1.3 ENERGY-EFFICIENT ROUTING PROTOCOLS IN WSN

WSNs are battery-operated devices. Therefore, an energy-efficient routing protocol is required. According to Ref. [5], routing protocol for WSNs is classified into four categories – network structure, topology-based, communication model and reliable routing as shown in Figure 1.1.

The first category is further divided into flat protocol and hierarchal protocols; second category into location-based and mobile agent-based; third category into query-based, coherent- and non-coherent-based, and negotiation-based; and fourth category into multipath-based and QoS-based protocols. Our research focus is on how protocols reduce the energy consumption and increase the network life span. Data sensing, data processing and data communication are the major factors that need to be considered while designing an energy-efficient routing protocol for WSN. However, data transmission and data reception require maximum energy; therefore, the main emphasis is on designing protocols that use less power in communication is given in the survey. Various performance parameters of routing protocols such as energy per packet, energy and reliability, network lifetime, average energy dissipation, low energy consumption, total number of alive nodes, total number of data signal received at BS, average packet delay, packet delivery ratio, time until the first node dies, energy spent per round, idle listening, packet size, and distance have

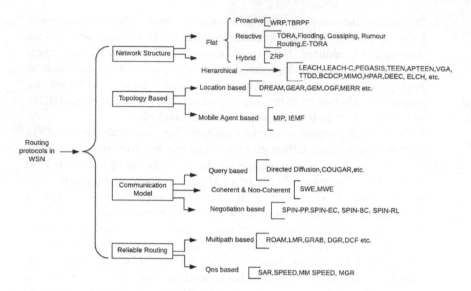

FIGURE 1.1   Routing protocols in WSNs.

also been discussed. Now, routing protocols in Ref. [7] are further distinguished as follows:

I. *Network structure-based routing protocol* – Nodes in the network are either uniformly distributed or randomly distributed. In this category, the nodes are either at similar level or at different levels of hierarchy. It is further classified as follows:

Flat protocol – In this scheme, all the nodes are of similar type. In trend, these protocols for WSNs can be divided, in step with the routing strategy, into three main distinctive categories: proactive, re-active and hybrid protocols [6]. Most of these protocols fluctuate in lots of methods and do not present the identical traits, even though they were designed for the same network.

Proactive routing protocol – Like wired network, in proactive protocols (or table-driven routing protocols), each node maintains its routing table to discover the route to the destination based on the intermittent exchange of routing messages between the specific nodes. Every node is required to preserve one or more tables with the help of routing records. In addition, nodes reply to various changes in network topology by wirelessly sending updates and appropriately retaining a regular network view. Consequently, direction to a few destinations, the packet will be forwarded through a predefined path, thereby avoiding time delay in path finding. However, to keep the data intact, heavy bandwidth and battery power is required which is always deficient and restrains the WSNs.

Reactive routing protocols – Unlike proactive protocols, it does not maintain a routing table, and it is available on-demand only. When the information needs to be transmitted from source to the destination, it is on request and searched at that time only. However, this process causes delays. But sometimes the routes are cached and need not to be discovered.

Hybrid routing protocol – Combining the advantages of both re-active and proactive routing protocols results in hybrid protocols. For local communication, that is nodes that are close to each other, it follows proactive routing protocol, and for inter-local communication, reactive routing protocol is used.

Hierarchical routing protocol – In hierarchical protocol, network is divided into clusters. Each cluster has a CH which has more energy as compared to other nodes in the cluster. So, despite directly sending the data to the sink, the nodes in the sensor network send data via CH to the BS and conserve energy. Since the data is aggregated before it is sent to the BS, the duplicate data is reduced in a dense network. More levels can be added to the clustering hierarchy. As the size of routing tables is drastically reduced in clustering, which increases the stability of the network.

Algorithms of hierarchical protocols – LEACH, HEED, PEGASIS, HPAR, MIMO, BCDCP, VGA, DEEC, etc. are the energy-efficient routing protocols, which will be discussed in detail in Section 2.4, as they are the basis of our research to achieve energy efficiency.

II. *Topology-based routing protocol* – This protocol assumes that all the nodes in the network know the topology information. It is classified into two parts:

Location-based protocol – In the location-based protocol, every node knows the location of its neighbor by sending the hello messages in the network. Since the location is known, it can send the data to a region; that is, sources can send the data to the destination since the location of the destination is known, thereby conserving energy. This protocol, which maintains location tables, is appropriate for mobile nodes.

Mobile agent based protocol – Mobile agent reduces the communication cost by moving the processing function to the data rather than bringing the data to a central processor. Mobile agents are used for efficient data dissemination in wireless sensor network.

1.4   HIERARCHICAL ROUTING PROTOCOLS

Hierarchical mechanism is one of the most efficient routing mechanisms as it increases the network life span and reduces the energy consumption [7]. In hierarchal routing, the sensed area is divided into clusters. A cluster head is allocated to each cluster, as shown in Figure 1.2. Sensor node senses the environment and sends the sensed data to the CH. CH aggregates the data received from multiple nodes.

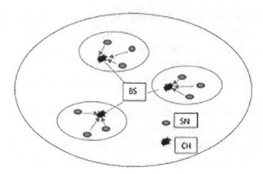

FIGURE 1.2   Clustering in WSN.

Then, the aggregated data is transmitted to the sink. Energy is required in formation of clusters as well as in selection of CHs. Cluster heads deplete their energy in receiving the data from sensor nodes, in data aggregation and in transmission of data to the sink. Therefore, CHs must be energy-efficient nodes because of their transmission and reception responsibilities. If CH nodes die quickly, the respective cluster is disconnected from the network and important events may be missed out. In this research, we have focused on achieving energy efficiency through optimal selection of cluster head as well as considering the residual energy concept for energy efficiency. Hierarchical routing protocol can be classified into two categories, as shown in Figure 1.2: as classical-based and meta-heuristic-based [8].

Authors in Ref. [9] emphasized on increasing the life span of network using homogeneous clustering algorithm. CHs are elected based on the residual energy of CH, holdback value, and nearest hop distance of the node. The homogeneous clustering algorithm extends the lifetime of network and maintains a balanced energy consumption of nodes. Cluster-based WSNs are classified into three main categories, which are given as follows:

Homogeneous sensor networks – Sensor nodes in the field are identical in terms of energy, processing power, hardware capabilities, etc.

Heterogeneous sensor networks – Sensor nodes are different in terms of battery power, processing power, hardware capabilities, security, etc.

Hybrid sensor networks – Sensor nodes are mobile, and they work together very fast to collect the data in a real-time manner. Hybrid networks can achieve longer lifetime and can also improve the efficiency of data gathering [10].

In the proposed method of CH selection, initially all the nodes have maximum energy and BS knows the location of all the nodes. Network is divided into random zones, and CH is selected for every zone but in a random fashion. There is a uniform distribution of sensor nodes. CHs collect the data from member nodes and send it to the BS. The next set of cluster heads is formed based on residual energy of the existing CHs. If it is less than the threshold value, a new CH is selected. The nodes that are closest to the existing CHs in terms of energy as well as hop distance should be selected as next CH. Since there is a uniform distribution of member nodes in the cluster, the power is saved and network life span is increased. But uniform distribution may not be feasible for all applications of WSN. Therefore, we consider heterogeneous network as well for our research work.

Researchers in Ref. [10] discussed the placement of heterogeneous nodes in the network to increase the network lifetime. Main emphasis is on how many number of heterogeneous nodes are deployed in the network, and the type and location where these nodes are deployed to increase the life of network. Three types of heterogeneous nodes are identified: computational nodes – nodes with added computational power; link heterogeneity nodes – nodes with highly reliable long-distance communication; and energy heterogeneity nodes – nodes with continuous energy resources. In this chapter, effective placement strategies and Mac-level support techniques are developed to find out the benefits of heterogeneous resources. Simulation and real test bed results show a positive impact of energy and link heterogeneity on the network. Optimal number of heterogeneous nodes or resources can increase the delivery rate and network life span.

1.4.1 CLASSICAL-BASED CLUSTERING PROTOCOLS

Classical routing conventions are those conventions which were essentially intended for mobile ad-hoc network; however, they are now being utilized for WSN. Despite the fact that it is suited for WSN applications, it has a great deal of difficulties like versatility and power. Classical routing techniques are utilized by sensor nodes or a base station autonomously.

A WSN has several battery-powered sensor nodes which transmit data, which is then aggregated and sent to a base station for further analysis. A very important objective in WSNs is to optimize overall energy consumption to increase the network lifetime. All the papers mentioned below propose different approaches to improve the energy conservation in WSNs. Different nodes are first clustered using a clustering algorithm, and then, a routing protocol is designed that is optimal for this cluster. The following papers propose either a modification of the clustering algorithm, routing procedure or both as compared to existing procedures. Much research has been done in the field of energy efficiency and has been reviewed in this section.

1.4.1.1 Centralized and Distributive Clustering

There are two types of clustering routing mechanism which needs to be considered before reviewing the protocols (Figure 1.3).

In centralized routing [11], the BS controls and manages the routing information. Sensors are aware of their location and therefore can be used by location aware sensors. The clusters and CH are determined by the BS. Single point failure can occur in this mechanism. Nodes function with global knowledge of the entire network, and any fault in transmission causes a serious critical failure of protocol.

Distributed algorithms function locally, within partial nodes, thereby preventing the failure caused by a single node. In distributed clustering algorithm, BS has no control on cluster formation and CH allocation to the clusters [12]. In this mechanism, sensor nodes are not aware of their location in the network, and routing

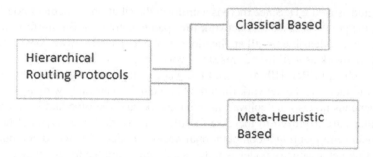

FIGURE 1.3 Classification of hierarchical routing protocol.

decision can be internally maintained. Clustering is performed by interacting with the peer nodes that consider the battery levels and node density. Localized clustering algorithms are more robust than centralized clustering algorithms, and they need not to wait for control messages to propagate across the network. This is suitable for dynamic networks.

Authors in Ref. [13] discussed low-energy adaptive clustering hierarchy (LEACH) protocol in which nodes in the network are divided into clusters. Nodes that are more proximate to the cluster head join the respective cluster only when they receive strong signal strength. Data transmits from nodes to the base station via cluster head, which are randomly chosen. Cluster head aggregates and compresses the data using different techniques and then forwards the data to the sink. Since CHs are randomly chosen, any node can get a chance to become a cluster head in the entire network. LEACH uses distributive clustering mechanism which consequently leads to efficient energy utilization and longer lifetime of the network. It consists of two phases: steady state and setup phase. In steady-state phase, sensor nodes join the cluster based on the signal strength received from the nearest CH. The TDMA slot has also been assigned to the sensor nodes in the cluster. In the steady-state phase, the sensor nodes send their sensed data to the CH in their respective slot, and then, CH sends the processed data to the base station. LEACH is not felicitous for large networks since nodes directly transmit data to the base station and cluster head. Enhancement in LEACH includes TL-LEACH [14], E-LEACH [15], M-LEACH [16], and LEACH-C [17]. Actual load balancing cannot be presented in LEACH. Also, dynamic clustering brings extra overhead.

Authors in Ref. [18] propounded threshold-sensitive energy-efficient sensor (TEEN) network protocol, which is a hierarchal protocol. TEEN discovered the instantaneous alterations within the sensed attribute, e.g., temperature which is important for time-relevant applications. It forms hierarchal grouping and uses data-centric mechanism. Neighboring nodes form clusters, and then, the different neighboring nodes form clusters. This process continues until the data reaches the sink. Cluster head broadcast two thresholds to the nodes: hard threshold (HT) and soft threshold (ST). HT is the perfect value of the attribute. Post this value, the node transmitter will switch on and announce to the cluster head. HT significantly reduces the transmission as it only transmits data above the threshold value, whereas ST senses small variations in attributes like temperature, which triggers the node, and sends the sensed data. The nodes will not communicate until the thresholds are not met. This protocol works for time critical data, like temperature, and is suitable for large networks. TEEN transmits only time crucial data, while keeping on sensing the environment, but it is not good for periodic reporting. It consumes energy because of long-distance transmission.

Researchers in Ref. [19] introduced power-efficient gathering in sensor information system (PEGASIS) protocol. It is a chain-based protocol in which nodes communicate to their next neighbor in the chain. A greedy algorithm approach is used to set up the sensor node chain, and the base station computes and broadcasts this chain to all sensor nodes. A single node in the chain is selected as the cluster head which transmits the data to the base station. Each node takes turns as the head of the chain, while transmitting the data to the sink. Therefore, load is evenly distributed among sensor nodes, and the energy consumption is reduced. Since no cluster formation takes place, there is a reduction in the overhead as compared to LEACH and a reduction in the energy consumption as well. In PEGASIS, all nodes must know the complete topology of the network to form the chain. As a result, scalability becomes an issue. Since the nodes communicate to the BS in chain, time-sensitive data are exposed to excessive delays. PEGASIS improves LEACH in terms of energy efficiency, but a single cluster head forms the bottle neck.

Authors Ref. in [20] have introduced distributed energy-efficient clustering (DEEC) algorithm for heterogeneous WSNs. In heterogeneous network, all nodes have different levels of energy, and the distributed nature of the network protects single point failure. In DEEC, like LEACH, the CH role is rotated among all the nodes in the network. CHs are chosen based on residual energy and average energy of the network. Nodes with high initial energy and residual energy have a high probability to become a CH. DEEC assigns different epoch for each round of selection of cluster head by considering both the initial energy and the residual energy. Residual energy is calculated on the basis of ideal value of a network lifetime, and global knowledge of the network is not required by each node. DEEC controls the equal dissipation of energy in each round by controlling the rotating epoch in accordance with the current energy level and average energy of the network as the reference energy. Hence, nodes die at the same time. DEEC results are more significant in terms of energy efficiency and longer lifetime of network compared to other algorithms. But advanced nodes are always punished to become CH. However after some rounds, the energy of advanced nodes is equal to that of normal nodes. Other limitation of DEEC is that the average energy is not directly proportional to the energy consumed in all iterations.

Authors in Ref. [21] depict selection process that considers both energy and topological features of the sensor nodes. Distributed energy-efficient clustering with improved coverage (DEECIC) is a distributed clustering algorithm which provides an efficient solution for large-scale networks. DEECIC can achieve re-clustering within a constant time and in a local manner. It deals with coverage preservation as compared to other traditional algorithms of maximum coverage. Coverage preservation is important particularly in dense areas, where if some nodes die, then it can be monitored by other nodes, but in a sparse area, problems may arise and some parts may not be monitored at all.

Researchers in Ref. [22] specify that energy consumption is particularly imbalanced for uneven node distribution in cluster-based WSNs. These authors propose both a clustering algorithm and a routing algorithm for the cluster, which they demonstrate to balance the energy expenditure across nodes and improve overall network lifetime. The proposed clustering algorithm, termed Energy Aware Distributed Clustering (EADC), is an alternative to existing algorithms such as LEACH, EADEEG and BPEC, which are an energy-aware multi-level clustering algorithm that constructs clusters of even sizes. But non-uniform node distribution leads to energy imbalance among cluster heads. The proposed routing algorithm uses energy-aware routing decisions to ensure the load balance among the nodes by making efficient trade-off between inter-cluster and intra-cluster energy consumption. That is, the cluster heads in sparse areas are compatible for more forwarding tasks. However, such testing was only carried out in a static network.

Authors in Ref. [23] have introduced H-DEEC for heterogeneous networks, and based on the residual energy of the sensor nodes, the network is logically divided in to two parts: normal nodes and beta nodes (high energy node for special purpose). This protocol considers the chain-based and cluster head selection mechanism for efficient energy utilization. Beta nodes are high energy nodes as compared to normal nodes. Clusters are formed out of normal nodes which is approximately 90% of the entire network, and remaining number of nodes becomes the beta nodes. Cluster head selection is based on DEEC considering the initial energy, residual energy and average energy of the network. Every node in the network is aware about the energy level and location of the nearest node.

Authors in Ref. [24] discussed a different approach to reduce the energy consumption, cost and complexity, by proposing a combination of routing algorithm and solar power, called as enhancement of energy conservation technology (EECT) in WSN. The use of solar power has not been very well accepted in the EECT literature and practice. However, these authors believe that there can be some specialized applications in large organizations that involve dealing with direct sunlight and heat. So, they propose tapping into solar energy for hot countries and for future purposes, to tap into wasted heat generated by the WSN devices themselves. Distance between the nodes and temperature of the node are two factors proposed by the authors to be taken into consideration in path selection criteria within the routing protocols. Comparison is made with SWAP, LEACH and DEESIC as energy conservation schemes (ECS), and simulations compare solar vs. ECS schemes.

Researchers in Ref. [25] demonstrated that CHSCDP algorithm gives an energy-efficient model for the selection of optimal cluster heads using an improved LEACH protocol, and this helps in increasing the lifetime of the network. Cluster heads are selected randomly by comparing their critical value, that is, distance, residual energy and number of rounds for being selected. CHSCDP uses the multi-hop communication, and for reducing energy consumption, unbalanced clustering is used. The nodes which are far away send the data to the CH which is nearest to the BS. The nearest CHs are kept smaller in size as it fuses the data of its own cluster and the faraway clusters, thus reducing the energy dissipation. For the inter-cluster communication, they use orthogonal variable spreading factor (OVSF) instead of TDMA because in TDMA, there is high energy consumption, total delay of the network is too large, and there is a requirement of synchronization at the starting of each round. It uses an improved mechanism based on OVSF for the communication between the cluster head and its cluster members. Indiscriminate data transmission is possible by studying the characteristics of orthogonality and incoherence of each node which reduces the delay and makes the whole network better at energy efficiency.

In simulation experiments between CHSCDP and LEACH, it can be easily seen that CHSCDP is better in every way:

- Minimum distance between cluster heads in CHSCDP is slightly greater than that in LEACH.
- CHSCDP also consumes very less energy than LEACH.
- The percentage of alive nodes is greater in comparison with LEACH.
- The residual energy is also greater in comparison with LEACH.
- Average delay can also be reduced by using CHSCDP instead of LEACH.
- In CHSCDP, more energy is consumed in the cluster formation phase.

Authors in Ref. [26] have discussed an energy-efficient DEEC protocol for enhancing the lifetime of WSN. This protocol has considered three-level node heterogeneity as hetDEEC-1, hetDEEC-2 and hetDEEC-3. Het1DEEC-1 and hetDEEC-2 are same because of the same energy level and number of nodes. Nodes are selected on the basis of weighted optimal probability of normal, advanced and super advanced node. This protocol outperforms the DEEC protocol in terms of prolonging the network lifetime.

1.4.2 Meta-Heuristic-Based Clustering Protocols

Many meta-heuristic search algorithms have been proposed by the researchers. Meta-heuristic means a "generalized local search"; heuristic means to search by hit and trial, and meta means beyond that or a higher level. Meta-heuristics are problem-independent methods that can be applied to a wide range of problems. A meta-heuristic algorithm can be applied to a problem without knowing anything about the problem. Meta-heuristic algorithms have been widely used in WSNs and have had a significant impact on the network lifetime. Swarm intelligence (SI)-based, ACO-based, Teaching Learning Based Optimization Algorithm (TLBO), Cuckoo search-based, genetic algorithm (GA), etc. clustering protocols are some modern meta-heuristic search algorithms [27].

SI is a meta-heuristic search technique characterized as "a natural model for algorithms designing or distributed problem solving inspired by the collective behavior of biological species, flock of birds or any social creature" [28]. Notwithstanding, these days SI alludes more by and large to the investigation of the collective behavior of multi-component frameworks that coordinate without any extra central control or coordination. From a building perspective, SI stresses the bottom-up plan of independent dispersed frameworks that can indicate versatile, scalable, and robust practices. The SI systems include other prominent structures, for example, ant colony optimization (ACO), particle swarm optimization (PSO) and GA. The majority of the work in the field of SI has been and still is motivated by collective behavior of species like ants or flock of birds and schools of fishes.

Author in Ref. [29] has propounded a load balancing, routing algorithm called Ant Colony Optimization (ACO) for WSN, where it used minimum spanning tree algorithm to develop intra-cluster routing and used the tree root as a CH initially. To attain the optimal route between the CH and destination sink, this algorithm is applied to inter-cluster routing. The results were favorable when compared with M-IAR and AGR with respect to end-to-end delay and regulation of energy.

Researchers in Ref. [30] have described a population-based algorithm and used the heuristic techniques. Unlike all other nature-inspired algorithm, TLBO does not have algorithm-specific control parameters but only the general parameters such as population size and total generations. It consists of two phases: (1) teaching phase and (2) learning phase. This concept simulates the classroom teaching environment where teacher is a knowledgeable person and wants to increase the knowledge of learners. The learner learns from teachers and enhances their knowledge. In learning phase, learner learns through interaction with each other. The learners are population, and their outcome is the fitness function of optimization problem. The best solution is considered as a teacher, and the design variables are objective function parameters. The best value of objective function is the best solution. This algorithm is used for many applications of engineering design. It is used in our proposed research for energy efficiency and network lifetime improvement.

Author in Ref. [31] has used a combination of two algorithms: GA and ACO to improve the network life and conserve the energy among sensor nodes. Here, the GA forms clusters and selects CH, while ACO finds the most efficient path between CH and the destination sink with the help of multi-path routing algorithm, which helps in creating an authentic communication in case the nodes fail within this route. The results show that this algorithm led to more energy conservation as compared to GABEEC and EEABR when simulated in MATLAB, with energy consumption with respect to time, per cycle, longevity and output of the network, as parameters.

Researchers in Ref. [32] have described a CH selection protocol based on PSO that takes into consideration residual energy and transmission distance. A fitness function is proposed which includes the function of energy dissipation due to intra-cluster communication and communication between CH and BS as well, in order to minimize the fitness function. The value of "pbest" and "gbest" is calculated, based on the evaluation of fitness function. The results when compared with LEACH and LEACH-C protocols show an improvement.

Authors in Ref. [33] have discussed a meta-heuristic algorithm named ICSCA (Improved Cuckoo Search-based Clustering Protocol for WSNs). In this protocol, a fitness function is devised which is based on cluster size, i.e., number of nodes in a cluster, residual energy of nodes, and distance between the CH and member node. Nodes which have the highest fitness values are considered as candidates for CH and cost of each eligible node is calculated. The node selected as a CH has the least cost based on average Euclidian distance (between nodes and CH) and ratio of total energy of all nodes to the total energy of all CHs. This algorithm when compared with LEACH, PSO-ECHS and E-OEERP shows significant improvement in the network lifetime.

1.5 EXPERIMENTAL REVIEW OF LEACH PROTOCOL

Low-energy adaptive clustering hierarchy (LEACH) is a well-accepted clustering routing protocol against which most of the papers benchmark their findings. The simulation of LEACH protocol is done to understand the concept of energy saving. It helped in finding out the various issues in LEACH in energy efficiency. The LEACH protocol is already discussed in Section 1.4.1 in detail.

1.5.1 SIMULATION OF LEACH

The simulation was done in MANNASIM framework. Different scenarios for different transmission range have been set, i.e., for 50 and 30 m. Network performance parameters taken into consideration are live nodes and average energy consumption. The simulation parameters are shown in Table 1.1.

1.5.2 SIMULATION RESULTS

Figure 1.4 shows the comparison of live nodes and number of cluster heads. It shows that the number of live nodes decreases as the number of cluster head varies. It also shows an increment for 6% of CHs and goes up to 8% of CH, and after that, number of live nodes again decreases.

Figure 1.5 shows the percentage of CH vs. number of CHs. As the number of cluster head increases, the average energy consumption increases as the number of live nodes decreases. But, the simulation results show an improvement in results for 8% of CH, and after that, energy consumption increases again.

Figure 1.6 shows the graph of live nodes with respect to the percentage of cluster heads for different scenarios. As the percentage of CH increases, the number of live nodes decreases except when CH is equal to 5%.

Figure 1.7 shows the variation of cluster heads with the average energy consumption. The energy consumption decreases as the percentage of CH increases.

TABLE 1.1
Simulation Parameters

S.#	Parameters	Values
1.	Numbers of nodes	100
2.	Scenario size	500×500 (m^2)
3.	Simulation time	500 s
4.	Base station location	50×175
5.	Transmission range	50 m
6.	% of cluster head	10, 12
7.	Initial energy	10 J
8.	Node distribution	Grid
9.	Min. packet in IFQ	50
10.	Antenna model	Antenna/omniAntenna

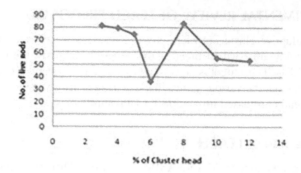

FIGURE 1.4   Percentage of cluster head vs. number of live nodes.

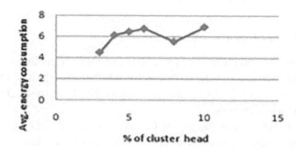

FIGURE 1.5   Percentage of cluster head vs. average energy consumption.

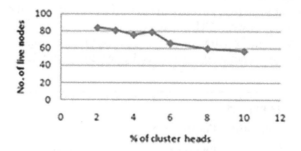

FIGURE 1.6   Percentage of cluster head vs. number of live nodes.

1.5.3   ANALYSIS OF LEACH PROTOCOL

It has been concluded that in LEACH, a number of cluster heads are presumed and increase/ decrease in number of cluster heads can increase the energy consumption. LEACH has not considered the optimal selection of cluster heads. Optimal selection of CH minimizes the energy consumption and increases the network life span. Since LEACH does not consider the residual energy for CH selection, the residual energy as well as the cluster head selection becomes the basis of our research (Table 1.2).

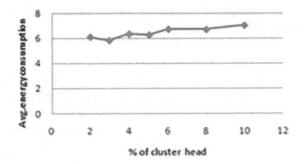

FIGURE 1.7 Percentage of cluster head vs. average energy consumption.

TABLE 1.2
Energy-Efficient-Based Clustering Protocols

Routing Protocol	Classification	Clustering Technique	Outcome/Limitations
LEACH [13]	Classical	Distributed	Random selection of CH, used for small networks
PEGASIS [19]	Classical	Distributed	Single CH forms bottleneck
TEEN [18]	Classical	Distributed	Not good for periodic data and large network
DEEC [20]	Classical	Distributed	Scalable but advanced nodes punished as CH continuously
DEECIC [21]	Classical	Distributed	Coverage preservation complex as unique ID for nodes is required
H-DEEC [23]	Classical	Distributed	Beta nodes for multi-hopping scheme with PEGASIS
hetDEEC [26]	Classical	Distributed	Three-level heterogeneity: hetDEEC-1, hetDEEC-2, and hetDEEC-3
	Classical	Distributed	Suitable for large networks, hierarchy of clusters, algorithm complexity
EADC [22]	Classical	Distributed	Clustering and routing protocol, load balancing achieved
EECT [24]	Classical	Distributed	Combines solar power and routing algorithm, limited to available sunlight space
CHSCDP [25]	Classical	Distributed	More energy is consumed in cluster formation phase
ICSCA [33]	Meta-heuristic	Distributed	Cluster head selects on avg. Euclidian distance and ratio of total energy to total energy of CH

(Continued)

TABLE 1.2 (*Continued*)
Energy-Efficient-Based Clustering Protocols

Routing Protocol	Classification	Clustering Technique	Outcome/Limitations
[32]	Meta-heuristic	Distributed	Cluster head selection protocol based on PSO based on residual energy and transmission distance
[29]	Meta-heuristic	Distributed	It used minimum spanning tree algorithm to develop intra-cluster routing and used the tree root as a CH
[31]	Meta-heuristic	Distributed	Use GA and ACO to improve network life, GA for clustering and CH selection and ACO for routing
TLBO [30]	Meta-heuristic	Distributed	Population-based method, no algorithmic-specific control parameters. Objective function gives the solution

1.6 SUMMARY

WSNs are an emerging area in which a number of sensor nodes are deployed to per-form the data gathering task. Sensor nodes are battery-based devices and therefore have limited power capacity. When the senor nodes are deployed in a remote area where human intervention is not feasible, the replacement or recharging of dead batteries is not possible. Power should be optimized carefully because less amount of power is available for a great deal of tasks such as transmission, reception, etc. Many sensor nodes are dispersed in the sensing field which sends the sensed data to the sink. Since the sensor nodes are deployed in close proximity of the sensing area, sensor nodes may send redundant data to the sink and consume more energy. The end user is interested in consolidated and non-redundant data. Therefore, with thorough literature survey, it has been found that hierarchical routing mechanism is one of the most efficient routing mechanisms. In WSN, the essential concern is energy proficiency, keeping in mind the end goal to expand the network utility. Our approach mainly focuses on the idea of maximizing the network lifetime based on CH nodes selection or CH nodes energy levels and hence contribution in green computing.

REFERENCES

1. Meghji, M. and Habibi, D., (2011). Transmission Power Control in Single-Hop and Multi-Hop Wireless Sensor Networks. *International Workshop on Multiple Access Communications-Springer*, ISSN: 03029743, pp. 130–143.
2. Pour, N.K., (2016). Energy Efficiency in Wireless Sensor Networks. *arXiv preprint-Cornell University Library*, arXiv:1605.02393, Research Report, pp. 1–158.

3. Enzinger, M., (2012). Energy-Efficient Communication in Wireless Sensor Networks. *Network Architectures and Services Seminar Proceedings*, ISSN: 18627811, pp. 25–31.
4. Soua, R. and Minet, P., (2011). A Survey on Energy Efficient Techniques in Wireless Sensor Networks. *4th Joint IFIP Wireless and Mobile Networking Conference (WMNC)*, ISBN:9781457711923, pp. 1–9. IEEE.
5. Pantazis, N.A., Nikolidakis, S.A. and Vergados, D.D., (2013). Energy-Efficient Routing Protocols in Wireless Sensor Networks: A Survey. *IEEE Communications Surveys & Tutorials*, Vol 15(2), ISSN: 1553877X, pp. 551–591.
6. Arce, P., Guerri, J.C., Pajares, A. and Lázaro, O., (2008). Performance Evaluation of Video Streaming Over Ad-hoc Networks Using Flat and Hierarchical Routing Protocols. *Mobile Networks and Applications Journal-Springer*, Vol 13(3–4), ISSN: 1383-469X, pp. 324–336.
7. Al-Karaki, J.N. and Kamal, A.E., (2004). Routing Techniques in Wireless Sensor Networks: A Survey. *IEEE wireless communications Journal*, Vol 11(6), ISSN: 1536-1284, pp. 6–28.
8. Zungeru, A.M., Ang, L.M. and Seng, K.P., (2012). Classical and Swarm Intelligence Based Routing Protocols for Wireless Sensor Networks: A Survey and Comparison. *Journal of Network and Computer Applications-Elsevier*, Vol 35(5), ISSN: 10848045, pp. 1508–1536.
9. Singh, S.K., Singh, M.P. and Singh, D.K., (2010). Energy-Efficient Homogeneous Clustering Algorithm for Wireless Sensor Network. *International Journal of Wireless & Mobile Networks (IJWMN)*, Vol 2(3), ISSN: 09754679, pp. 49–61.
10. Yarvis, M., Kushalnagar, N., Singh, H., Rangarajan, A., Liu, Y. and Singh, S., (2005). Exploiting Heterogeneity in Sensor Networks. *INFOCOM 2005. 24th Annual Joint Conference of the IEEE Computer and Communications Societies. Proceedings IEEE*, Vol-2, ISBN: 0780389689, pp. 878–890.
11. Zanjireh, M.M. and Larijani, H., (2015). A Survey on Centralized and Distributed Clustering Routing Algorithms for WSNs. *81st Vehicular Technology Conference (VTC Spring)-IEEE*, ISSN: 15502252, pp. 1–6.
12. Shigei, N., Miyajima, H., Morishita, H. and Maeda, M., (2009). Centralized and Distributed Clustering Methods for Energy Efficient Wireless Sensor Networks. *Proceedings of the International Multi Conference of Engineers and Computer Scientists (IMECS)*, Vol 1, ISBN:9789881701220, pp. 18–20.
13. Heinzelman, W.R., Chandrakasan, A. and Balakrishnan, H., (2000). Energy-Efficient Communication Protocol for Wireless Microsensor Networks. *Proceedings of the 33rd annual Hawaii International Conference on System Sciences*, ISBN: 0769504930, pp. 1–10.
14. Loscri, V., Morabito, G. and Marano, S., (2005). A Two-Level Hierarchy for Low-Energy Adaptive Clustering Hierarchy (TL-LEACH). *IEEE Vehicular Technology Conference*, Vol 62(3), ISSN: 0780391527, pp. 1809–1813.
15. Xiangning, F. and Yulin, S., (2007). Improvement on LEACH Protocol of Wireless Sensor Network. *International Conference on Sensor Technologies and Applications, Sensor Comm 2007*, ISBN: 0769529887, pp. 260–264.
16. Mhatre, V. and Rosenberg, C., (2004). Homogeneous Vs Heterogeneous Clustered Sensor Networks: A Comparative Study. *International Conference on Communications-IEEE*, Vol 6, ISBN: 0780385330, pp. 3646–3651.
17. Tilak, S., Abu-Ghazaleh, N.B. and Heinzelman, W., (2002). A Taxonomy of Wireless Micro-Sensor Network Models. *ACM SIGMOBILE Mobile Computing and Communications Review*, Vol 6(2), ISSN: 15591662, pp. 28–36.
18. Manjeshwar, A. and Agrawal, D.P., (2001). TEEN: A Routing Protocol for Enhanced Efficiency in Wireless Sensor Networks. *15th International Parallel and Distributed Processing Symposium-IEEE*, Vol 03, ISBN: 0769509908, pp. 2009–2015.

19. Lindsey, S. and Raghavendra, C.S., (2002). PEGASIS: Power-Efficient Gathering in Sensor Information Systems. *Aerospace Conference Proceedings- IEEE*, Vol. 3, ISBN: 078037231, pp. 1125–1130.
20. Qing, L., Zhu, Q. and Wang, M., (2006). Design of A Distributed Energy-Efficient Clustering Algorithm for Heterogeneous Wireless Sensor Networks. *Journal of Computer Communications-Elsevier*, Vol 29(12), ISSN: 01403664, pp. 2230–2237.
21. Liu, Z., Zheng, Q., Xue, L. and Guan, X., (2012). A Distributed Energy-Efficient Clustering Algorithm with Improved Coverage in Wireless Sensor Networks. *Future Generation Computer Systems Journal*, Vol 28(5), ISSN: 0167739X, pp. 780–790.
22. Yu, J., Qi, Y., Wang, G. and Gu, X., (2012). A Cluster-Based Routing Protocol for Wireless Sensor Networks with Non-Uniform Node Distribution. *AEU-International Journal of Electronics and Communications*, Vol 66(1), ISSN: 14348411, pp. 54–61.
23. Khan, M.Y., Javaid, N., Khan, M.A., Javaid, A., Khan, Z.A. and Qasim, U., (2013). Hybrid DEEC: Towards Efficient Energy Utilization in Wireless Sensor Networks. *arXiv.org, preprint:1303.4679-Cornell University Library*, pp. 1–15.
24. Thayananthan, V. and Alzranhi, A., (2014). Enhancement of Energy Conservation Technologies in Wireless Sensor Network. *Procedia Computer Science- Elsevier*, Vol 34, ISSN: 18770509, pp. 79–86.
25. Qiang, Y., Pei, B., Wei, W. and Li, Y., (2015). An Efficient Cluster Head Selection Approach for Collaborative Data Processing in Wireless Sensor Networks. *International Journal of Distributed Sensor Networks*, Vol 11(6), ISSN: 15501477 Art.Id-794518. pp. 1–9.
26. Singh, S., Malik, A. and Kumar, R., (2017). Energy Efficient Heterogeneous DEEC Protocol for Enhancing Lifetime in WSNs. *Engineering Science and Technology, An International Journal- Elsevier*, Vol 20(1), ISSN: 22150986, pp. 345–353.
27. Sorensen, K., Sevaux, M. and Glover, F., (2017). A History of Metaheuristics. *arXiv Preprint -Cornell University Library*, arXiv:1704.00853, Springer, pp. 1–27.
28. Saleem, M., Di Caro, G.A. and Farooq, M., (2011). Swarm Intelligence Based Routing Protocol for Wireless Sensor Networks: Survey and Future Directions. *Information Sciences-Elsevier*, Vol 181(20), ISSN: 00200255, pp. 4597–4624.
29. Bi, J., Li, Z. and Wang, R., (2010). An Ant Colony Optimization-Based Load Balancing Routing Algorithm for Wireless Multimedia Sensor Networks. *12th IEEE International Conference on Communication Technology (ICCT)*, ISBN: 9781424468713, pp. 584–587.
30. Rao, R.V., Savsani, V.J. and Vakharia, D.P., (2011). Teaching–Learning-Based Optimization: A Novel Method for Constrained Mechanical Design Optimization Problems. *Computer-Aided Design-Elsevier*, Vol 43(3), ISSN: 00104485, pp. 303–315.
31. Wagh, S. and Das, S., (2014). Prolonging the Lifetime of the Wireless Sensor Network Based on Blending of Genetic Algorithm and Ant Colony Optimization. *Journal of Green Engineering*, Vol 4(3), ISSN: 19044720, pp. 245–260.
32. Yadav, R.K., Kumar, V. and Kumar, R., (2015). A Discrete Particle Swarm Optimization Based Clustering Algorithm for Wireless Sensor Networks. *Emerging ICT for Bridging the Future-Proceedings of the 49th Annual Convention of the Computer Society of India CSI*, Vol-2, ISBN: 9783319137308, pp. 137–144.
33. Gupta, G.P., (2018). Improved Cuckoo Search-Based Clustering Protocol for Wireless Sensor Networks. *Procedia Computer Science (Elsevier)*, ISSN: 18770509, Vol 125, pp. 234–240.

2 Challenges and Opportunities with Green and Sustainable Computing in Healthcare

Anam Saiyeda
Jamia Hamdard

CONTENTS

2.1 INTRODUCTION

The pervasive power of the Internet has given almost everyone access to mobile devices in the form of not just mobile phones but also smart watches, and other wearable devices embedded by sensors. Use of such devices with sensors like the accelerometer and gyroscope along with the availability of a wide variety of apps for physical as well as mental health being has made it easier to monitor our health. Development in ubiquitous computing and embedded devices as well as use of sensors brings down the cost of hardware and equipment needed for health monitoring. Thus, technology has helped healthcare have a wider reach and be available to a wider range of people. The applications of IOT in healthcare leading to e-health and m-health can be broadly classified based on the type of health condition targeted, i.e., patient care (chronic diseases and communicable diseases), medicine adherence,

19

caretakers help, and direct contact with doctors, health monitoring, etc. Apart from these, we have the sectors of pharmaceutical industry and independent living. IT has wide applications ranging from assistance in clinical care, real-time health status, remote monitoring of patients in rural and urban areas, helping chronic disease patients in self-care by enabling adherence, post-treatment communication, etc. All these have led to reduction in the dependency of patients on medical equipment and doctors leading to better healthcare. Green computing attempts to effectively utilize computing assets. Computational devices ranging from smart phones, laptops, wearable devices, tablets, to huge servers all have some amount of energy consumption.

Better healthcare leads to economic growth, thus satisfying 3 out of 17 goals of sustainable development, i.e., number 3, which refers to good health and well-being, number 8 to economic growth and number 11 to sustainable cities and communities. Green computing is being used in healthcare with sustainable tactics, which include data center outsourcing and collocation. Hospitals are becoming smart to reduce wastage and practice sustainability. There is an opportunity to bridge the remaining gap between current sustainable usage and the optimal usage and leading to improved efficiency and decline in cost. Power management software, telecommuting and telemedicine are some of the ways to encourage green computing as well as sustainable practices in the area of healthcare. The challenges faced include managing huge quantities of data of all types structured, semi-structured, as well as unstructured, which is amplifying at an "exponential rate," moving from volume to value, integrating sensors, monitors and instruments in real time, making hospitals smarter at the same time as making them greener.

This chapter begins with the applications of IoT and other technologies promoting green computing such as cloud, edge and fog computing in the healthcare sector. Then, the strategies to enable green and sustainable computing in healthcare sector are discussed. This is followed by a roadmap to get to this by the use of IoT and similar computing practices. At the end, the challenges faced during this are discussed followed by a case study.

2.2   APPLICATIONS OF TECHNOLOGY IN THE HEALTHCARE SECTOR

Technology and computing is nowadays being used in every realm of life. In the healthcare sector, IoT, big data, cloud computing, machine learning, edge and fog computing have found a lot of applications and uses leading to the development of sub-fields of health analytics, IoT (IoHT, IoMT), computer-aided design (CAD), e-health, m-health, robotic surgery, etc. Health informatics (HI) also known as health information systems is a field which involves the various disciplines of computer science and healthcare such as data analytics and image processing. It deals with the devices, techniques and measures for optimizing the acquisition, repository, retrieval and "use of information in health and biomedicine."

The use of computers in medicine began as early as the 1950s. Automation of the financial and accounting functions was the first task performed by them. From that to the ECG-enabled Apple watch technology has come a long way. The focus has now shifted to e-health and m-health technologies in the healthcare sector.

Electronic health records (EHRs) was the first step in digitalization of the field of healthcare. Digital records ensured availability of health information of patients which further led to the improvement of patient care and public health. In this, all the data about a patient is present, and it becomes easier to observe any abnormal behavior, thus resulting in quicker diagnosis. The field of remote patient monitoring has been very beneficial in healthcare applications. Internet of Things (IoT), cloud computing, machine learning, and big data are the popular Information and Communication Technology (ICT) paradigms, which are shaping the next generation of e-health and m-health systems.

The discussion begins with the sector, which has immense applications in healthcare field, i.e., ubiquitous computing, which involves IoT and edge computing. This has been widely implemented in health monitoring system. The IoT has been created by the ubiquitous deployment of mobile and sensor devices. These may include self-monitoring of everyday activities through the use of sensors in mobile phones, smart watches for lifestyle monitoring, remote patient monitoring and treatment adherence in chronic disorders or mental ailments. Technology makes patients and elderly become independent and not require the help of their relatives or caregivers. This can be made possible by continuous monitoring and alerting mechanisms [1]. Their applications can be categorized into chronic disorder treatment, mental health monitoring and treatment adherence, lifestyle monitoring, remote patient monitoring to get their physiological status and hospital management. For chronic disorders and elderly care, cloud-based e-health platform has been discussed by [2]. Remote health monitoring of elderly has been carried out by the use of sensors [3]. Cloud technology has also been combined with IoT for remote monitoring [4]. For chronic disorder management like asthma [5] and such other diseases, these have been applied. For mental health, stress management [6], fog and mobile computing techniques have been applied. Medical treatment is now being combined with intelligent systems to get precision medicine. Telemedicine is another medical care practice that has found great use of computing techniques for its wider applications. It includes not just medical care delivery and health education but also consultation, electronic medical record (EMR), diagnosis and treatment. IoT has enabled implementation of deep and rich communication and interaction by multimedia between patients and specialists even from remote areas.

Biomedical systems are another area with increased use of electronic and computing devices. Implantable devices are electronic devices which monitor the user's physiological parameters. They can replace the biological functions of the human body. Cochlear implants and pacemakers are two examples of such medical devices. Green computing needs to ensure that energy dissipation of devices is minimal. Implantable devices need continuous energy sources and efficient thermal management, along with no compromise in quality. Biomedical servers need renewable energy sources.

Biomedical implantable devices have issues of heat dissipation along with generated electromagnetic fields. To reduce this thermal management is one approach. Another way would be efficient design of the algorithm along with the microchip of the device. This causes reduced amount of power consumption by the device. The power consumed can be reduced significantly by using compact code and having

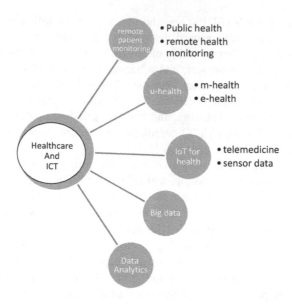

FIGURE 2.1 Use of ICT in healthcare.

efficient operations. A huge amount of biomedical systems nowadays utilize embedded platforms. Their applications range from physiological monitoring systems and the likes of recognition systems. Migrating the computations of these systems from traditional servers to embedded platforms can lead to better energy consumption.

Some embedded biotelemetry systems monitor patient's physiological parameters (e.g., weight and blood pressure) along with location and use Bluetooth to transmit data from device to embedded system. Embedded processors perform the basic tasks and transmit data to the centralized processing units. WBANs are also used for providing healthcare services. The increased use of technology in healthcare also generates huge amount of data, which leads to developments in the fields of big data and machine learning. Medical records of patients, hospital records, results and reports of medical examinations are the sources of data. For smarter healthcare, many techniques and architectures for analysis of this data have been provided in the big data field [7,8].

Figure 2.1 shows a graphical representation of the various sectors where ICT has found applications in healthcare. This shows the fields of u-health, big data, remote patient monitoring, etc.

2.3 STRATEGIES TO ENABLE GREEN AND SUSTAINABLE COMPUTING IN THE HEALTHCARE SECTOR

The last decade has seen a digital revolution and exponential rise in the usage of Internet-based services. This has led to amplified energy consumption. IT and computing are now being used in the healthcare sector. This means augmented usage by individuals, hospitals, clinics and healthcare professionals, leading to rising power consumption. This is because all these techniques are powered by the Internet.

The data center power consumption in the years 2005 to 2010 grew at an unsustainable rate of 24% [9].

The issues of energy and sustainability often arise in the sectors of manufacturing, civil, transport and petroleum industries. However, computing and IT techniques are big contributors to high energy consumption, negative environmental effects and carbon emissions. They need to facilitate green environmental conventions, processes and habits in everyday operations, and reduce the carbon footprint and energy consumption. Thus, there is a need to redefine the existing practices, hardware and algorithms for energy proficient activities and sustainable operations so as to reduce environmental hazards caused by this energy consumption. Green techniques are implemented in order to achieve this goal.

The paper [9] defined green computing as utilizing computing resources in an efficient manner which minimizes their environmental impact. The Green Lights program introduced in 1992 by The Environmental Protection Agency (EPA) was the first step towards green practices. It aims to maximize IT resource efficiencies and encourage the reuse of resources (particularly energy). Another aim is to adopt sustainable, renewable and feasible products, along with manufacturing practices and support green practices, innovations and initiatives in other industries too. ICT and green computing are two concepts which cannot be un-coupled. Green computing, green ICT or ICT sustainability attempts to attain environmentally sustainable computing or IT. Every technology-driven system from simple websites, handheld systems to large-scale data centers need to practice sustainable and green practices with the growing climate and environment issues. In the past few years, technological and digital revolution has grown immensely. In every walk of life, there is infiltration of technology, and ubiquitous and pervasive computing is on the rise. Healthcare is another such field which utilizes technology and computing in a huge manner. Sustainability may be supported by the ICT systems in a wide assortment of mechanisms. ICT could be used to monitor the effect of other systems (e.g., buildings and transportation) to measure their impact on the environment, check their sustainability and promote green-aware decisions. Another way could be designing efficient ICT systems which contribute in declining the energy expenditure associated with ICT itself. Green computing technologies may encompass several fields including cloud computing, IoT, fog computing, sustainable computer architecture and hardware design. We discuss one by one how green computing can be incorporated in these.

2.3.1 GREEN AND SUSTAINABLE COMPUTING IN THE CLOUD

Green Cloud Architecture helps multiple applications in various data centers manage on-demand resource provisioning in a manner which reduces power consumption. Energy-efficient management of resources is required for mobile devices, servers, data centers, etc. "Cloud data centers" (CDCs) offer a variety of utilities such as "high-performance computing," unlimited storage, fast processing, and large-scale data analytics. Thus, cloud-based services and applications need a large number of data centers[10]. Advancements in computational power lead to huge amount of electrical power consumption. These centers will have thousands of web servers, network devices, and storage. Various CDCs have been established by the providers, at several different geographical locations to provide this massive amount of resources. The servers use a rack-mounted design leading to soaring energy expenditure, along with heat dissipation, leading to rise in energy demands of these data centers in the form of direct energy and indirect cooling [11]. Cloud computing can provide sustainable distributed computing by blending it with definite characteristics available from other technologies. Cloud computing model allows reduction of the power and energy consumption without investing money on setting up, running and maintaining the servers. Without server maintenance and repair, there are no hardware to upgrade and software installation and maintenance, which results in reduced labor costs. With SaaS accessible through browsers, it makes desktop and laptop resources replaceable. Cloud computing also helps reduce costs and increases green role in business. This is because it decreases traveling and moving costs of employees from various locations by allowing remote access. Reducing traveling reduces the consumption of fossil fuels and also thus reduces the pollution resulting from vehicle emissions.

Grid computing's distributed resource provision, sustainability from green computing and distributed control of digital ecosystems can be utilized along with the cloud. Further green infrastructure can lead to economic and environmental sustainability. Data centers of cloud can be made environment-friendly. The "green" cloud data center has three broad classifications: resource management, sustainability with renewable energy and waste heat utilization, and resource scheduling [12]. Resource management techniques are further classified into three sub-fields: resource scheduling, migration and load balancing [13]. Resource scheduling is the first resource management technique which involves the scheduling of suitable resources to their cloud workloads. Scheduling is done on the basis of cost, time, performance and reliability. Some of the algorithms used are time-cost scheduling algorithm [14], workflow scheduling algorithm [15], improved cost-based algorithm for task scheduling [16], and so on. Nature-inspired algorithms like genetic algorithm (GA), particle swarm optimization (PSO), simulated annealing algorithm (SA), and ant colony optimization can be applied for resource management problems in cloud computing data centers for energy management [17].

Load balancing refers to the distribution of workloads over numerous computing resources. Load balancing for cloud should be done in a way to maximize availability of resources while keeping cloud networks energy efficient. Load-balancing techniques should be designed in a way to consider resource utilization, performance, throughput, scalability and fault tolerance which are related to energy consumption and energy reduction in data centers of cloud to make green cloud. Virtual machine (VM) migration is done in case of a faulty server. The migrating VM can be allocated to any of the several servers. Migration should be done to a server that consumes least energy, on hosting the VM to ensure green practices. Apart from data centers, several other approaches can be taken to go for sustainable green computing. The basic one could be research on techniques to modify the software development life cycle (SLDC) in order to minimize the prospective harmful environmental degradation caused and the carbon footprint. Knowledge management, environmental impact measurement and periodic reporting are some practices to enable environmental sustainability. At the time of design of new products, environmental parameters should be taken into account.

Another way to achieve green computing is sustainability in operations. Renewable energy resources such as solar power and wind energy should be used for cloud data centers to reduce emissions. Reuse of resources is another useful technique for sustainability. Servers have high cooling requirements utilizing electricity. The waste heat generated can be reused for other purposes like heating in homes and offices. Data center design should be done in a way to ensure green techniques like setting them up in cold geographic locations, which automatically cuts down the cooling requirements. There are many non-technical practices which should be followed by the cloud service provider in order to follow green norms. One simple practice is building data centers at such locations where the environment is cold to reduce the costs of cooling down machines and servers. Designing of buildings should be done in an energy efficient manner. Factors like the weather impact the green practices. Use of renewable energy resources for power requirements is another. Location of centers should be such that renewable energy resources are nearby. These small factors have a huge impact on the environment. An example is Microsoft's data center, which has been built in central Washington. This is because it can utilize the hydroelectric power coming from the nearby located dams. They have another data center in Ireland (the climate there is moderate) which is air-cooled. Green cloud computing can be studied under various categories such as models and methods, frameworks, architectures, algorithms and general issues. Another approach for reducing power consumption of cloud and having energy-efficient data centers is by introducing nanodata centers. These are distributed computing-based platforms. The basic idea of NaDa is having huge amounts of data centers. They have smaller size than the general data centers. They are distributed geographically and are interconnected. Usual data centers are larger in size. These data centers consume lesser amount of energy. Some more approaches used for green cloud practices can include Greedy Minimum Carbon Emission (GMCE). Here based on the user's carbon emissions, the user applications are assigned to the cloud providers. Others include assigning applications to the cloud provider with minimum carbon emission due to the location of their data center and also application execution.

2.3.2 GREEN AND SUSTAINABLE COMPUTING IN BIG DATA

Healthcare applications generate a massive amount of data from sensors, devices and EMRs in the form of text, images and videos. Big data has various applications along with cloud computing and analytics. It has volume, velocity and variety. Data is of large size and needs fast input and output. For handling this data, there is a need of "massively parallel processing (MPP) databases, scalable storage systems," servers, and "fog and cloud computing platforms." Big data, machine learning, and data analysis and analytics require not only massive amounts of hardware processing, and scalable and efficient storage space but also a lot of computing power, electricity and high availability of main memory. So green big data practices are the need of the hour to reduce the carbon footprints of big data techniques. Green big data analytics can be divided into three realms broadly: based on hardware, infrastructure and algorithms.

In the energy domain, big data processing systems need green infrastructure, green design and development, and sustainable and green data centers as discussed above to reduce the environmental problems caused by its storage and processing in data centers. Design of such sustainable and environment friendly components will lead to green hardware and infrastructure. Monitoring/optimization of complex electro-mechanical systems (used in health monitoring) needs to be done to track the environmental impacts. Hazardous impact on the environment can be reduced by monitoring of energy flow on transmission and distribution grids (smart metering). Forecasting of energy demand can avoid wastage of resources. Usage of renewable energy production leads to green production. Big data utilizes cloud-based resources, so green cloud computing practices will automatically lead to green and sustainable big data. Green-cloud computing techniques discussed in the previous sections cover the field of making data centers green and resource scheduling. Here, we discuss the other ways to make big data green. Green big data analytics will need infrastructure scalability, efficient resource utilization and energy consumption. Other unconventional ways to utilize big data need to be thought; i.e., smart cars could generate information that could be analyzed to find out the greenest routes, recharging patterns and driving techniques. In the algorithm field, there is a need to design green algorithms for analyzing healthcare big data. This can be done by designing algorithms and programs in such a way so as to optimize the energy consumption of the given code.

In order to make the task of healthcare big data processing green and sustainable, the concept of Green Hadoop [18] was introduced. It is a MapReduce framework for data centers. The centers are driven by solar energy, and a backup electrical grid is available. It is used for predicting the quantity of solar energy that will be accessible in the future, and schedules the MapReduce jobs accordingly to maximize the green energy consumption within the jobs' time bounds. It is also used for finding when brown energy is the cheapest, and at peak, brown power consumption controls the cost. Compared to Hadoop, it significantly decreases electricity cost and increases green energy consumption. GreenPlum [19] is a database which introduced cost-based query optimization. It is a MPP database server. It ensures usage efficiency while performing analytics on large volume data sets. Its architecture is specially designed to manage large-scale analytic data warehouses as well as the business intelligence workloads. It handles volume well, as for "multi-terabyte data warehouses" it can distribute the load easily. To process a query, it can utilize all of a system's resources in parallel, thus ensuring efficiency in execution. The algorithms used can also contribute to energy consumption and green practices. An example is Google's DeepMind, which is an artificial intelligence implementing machine learning algorithms and enables the company to get minimal amount of energy consumption used for cooling. Similarly, more such tools and techniques need to be developed which lead to more green practices.

2.3.3 GREEN AND SUSTAINABLE COMPUTING IN IoT

IoT has the power to enhance the connectivity of everyone, everything, everywhere. IoT has brought about many changes in the healthcare field. It enhances traditional and conventional medical devices by enhancing their feature with addition of sensors and networking features. Intelligent interaction between patients, health workers and devices has been made possible. With the increased usage of mobile devices and the introduction of smart phones, the field of IoMT has developed, i.e., Internet of Medical Things. It is also known as healthcare IoT. IoMT has empowered the health industry and enabled health facilities to reach remote locations. This is because mobile devices are now easily available at low costs and are available everywhere. Medical devices and applications constitute the IoMT, which are connected to the healthcare IT systems. These include remote patient monitoring, medication-tracking systems, wearable devices, smart watches and sensor-enabled hospital beds. Thus, IoT has made healthcare mobile and easily accessible. Green computing is very important for the field of IoT because of increased usage of IoT devices. IoT technology needs to be changed in order to move towards green IoT procedures in the form of hardware effective or software efficiency approaches. Medical and healthcare can be made smart, sustainable and green, by introducing energy-efficient methods in medical IoT (MIoT) systems. Diminution of the greenhouse effect, energy efficiency in the existing operation and methods are the goals of green IoT. Green design and redesign, green productions and green recycling/disposal are some of the practices adopted in this paradigm. Green MIoT systems should have energy-saving sensors and devices like batteries. Energy harvesting or energy scavenging takes benefit of the ambient power sources which incorporate motion, heat, and light. Battery-powered devices demonstrate energy profligacy. Their idle time is longer than the time of use. In healthcare, sensors need continuous execution for monitoring of health. Thus, new and energy-harvesting technologies must be applied to them to avoid use of such batteries which lead to environment issues. EnOcean company has range of products for IoT applications that depend on the energy harvesting to provide them the source of power. Energy saving can be applied to WBSNs. The wearable nodes/devices should be designed and energy investment done in a way to extend the lifetime of each device and thus of the whole network. Another way to ensure green IoT is to implement reuse of devices. Green disposal of devices will ensure lesser impact on the environment.

Some of the communication strategies and technologies for green and sustainable IoT are green wireless sensor network (GWSN), green radio-frequency identification (GRFID) and green machine-to-machine communication (GM2MC). It will also include the practices of context-aware green networks, green services in IoT, opportunistic routing protocols, green localization in IoT, green communications and green network architecture design and green mobile computing. Green design approach should be followed while designing medical IoT devices. The design of medical IoT devices in medical healthcare applications should pay attention to energy and charge dissipation problems. This can be achieved by energy and battery-efficient algorithms for green healthcare. With ubiquitous computing growing at a fast pace massive amount of devices, sensors will be surrounding us. Green support will have to be provided for them. Ubiquitous devices will lead to u-healthcare and will be context-aware, and have the capability to perform certain autonomous functions. This will develop green communication between user and devices and between devices with optimized power consumption and maximum bandwidth utilization.

GRFID can be obtained by the help of green design. Reduction in the size of RFID tag size will make recycling easier. Green manufacturing can be achieved by reducing the non-degradable material while tag manufacturing. The use of communication algorithms can help in energy optimized and green communication. The protocols for implementing energy efficiency can also help achieve this aim. These both work by adjustment of the intensity of transmission power and techniques for optimization. GWSN can be created for optimizing the energy usage in WSN. This can be done by replacing continuous monitoring with periodic updates and timestamp-less synchronization. GM2MC can be obtained by improving energy efficiency by astute change of the transmission power to the required intensity, using energy-efficient routing protocols and energy harvesting techniques, and scheduling the activity in the machine domain [20]. Green media-aware MIoT is another step towards less power consumption while providing clearer picture of patients and physician along with a long-lasting communication [21].

Hospitals should also be made in such a way so, as to have smart building management. This can be done by using renewable energy resources to power it, thus reducing consumption of electricity and power. Then, the monitoring of amount of resources used must be done to avoid wastage. Sensors, devices, infrastructure, etc. should be designed to obtain green hospitals.

2.3.4 GREEN AND SUSTAINABLE COMPUTING AT HARDWARE AND SOFTWARE LEVELS

At the core level, green computing can be introduced for the hardware, architecture, network and the devices used for healthcare IT methodologies and solutions. A large amount of energy is consumed by hardware devices, systems, network devices, etc. Apart from making data centers green, we need to introduce some mechanisms to make other devices in healthcare settings such as desktops used in hospitals, network devices and softwares also sustainable and green. Green network through energy-efficient network technologies, protocols and products can help reduce the carbon footprints to a great extent. Energy cost savings of a single device may seem small, but on a larger scale, when combining thousands of devices, it is not negligible. Small changes like the use of newer, green and energy-efficient techniques, technologies and products can help green computing a lot. Update and replace older devices with newer, greener network devices. At a small level, wherever possible thin clients can replace larger systems to save energy. Hospitals, data centers, etc. should use Energy Star-certified devices. Given a ratio of off, sleep and idle states, Energy Star-certified machines follow a yearly energy consumption threshold. The move to green IT in the form of utilization of virtualization will enable hospitals and healthcare outlets in minimizing the equipment price and system management costs.

Virtualization in the form of server virtual data storage technology can be utilized for this. Private cloud computing for production and test/development systems will lead to more savings. Other methods include the use of intelligent systems, greening scan applied to systems, data storage, user management, taking green storage considerations into account when buying storage hardware and energy conservation through networks to improve energy efficiency, and the use of remote management and videoconferencing instead while traveling. Energy-efficient networks can be obtained by having energy-efficient protocols for routing, medium access, hand-off and adaptive link rate (ALR) techniques. The goal of green computing has led to the introduction of various new methods like zero-configuration networking (zeroconf). Apple has a component of zero-configuration networking called Bonjour Sleep Proxy [22]. It assists networked electronic devices in reducing their power consumption. Other implementations of zeroconf are also available like Avahi for Linux and BSDs, MS Windows CE 5.0, systemd and BusyBox. The concept of thin client sleep proxies and dynamic virtual machine migration also work towards this goal. Improvements in the energy competence of networking technologies include the software and virtualization techniques such as software-defined networking (SDN) and network function virtualization (NFV). The SDN supports energy-efficient network operations via the pervasive programmable interface. It implements green computing policies at the network level. NFV is a technique used in telecommunication systems. It helps in obtaining energy efficiency by decoupling network functions from physical devices. One green methodology that is hardware oriented is the dynamic voltage and frequency scaling (DVFS) technology. DVFS is an approach, which controls CPU power consumption. This is done by the use of wide operating range of CMOS digital circuits. Another approach is the design and use of devices like the Intel Atom. It is an ultra-low-voltage x86 processor which was designed using 45 nm CMOS technology. Mobile platforms are its main consumers. Similarly, the NVidia Tegra APX 2500 chip includes an ARM11 600 MHz MPCore processor along with ultra-low-power NVIDIA graphics processing unit (GPU). It finds use in devices like mobile phones, which have low-power applications. Apple A5, Samsung Exynos 4210, AMD Fusion, IBM PowerPC 476FP, etc. are some other hardware devices designed to be energy efficient and reduce power consumption to make technologies green [27]. Fast Array and Wimpy Nodes are another way of achieving green computing. It is a cluster system, which has low power consumption capability. It is used for large-scale data-intensive applications and intensive input/output tasks. Service shutdown is another way to achieve green techniques goals. This is done by automating the switching/powering off of the system and the hardware components or network after some kind of failure. Manual intervention may be required in this. This leads to energy conservation.

2.4   ROADMAP FOR HEALTHCARE SETTINGS FOR GREEN PRACTICES

Everyone in the healthcare setting from hospitals, healthcare centers, to workers including doctors as well as other staff and users should be included in the process of making computing in this sector green and sustainable. The healthcare sector has moved towards digitalization at every level. Technology is now being used at every step. From data entry and record keeping of patients, health monitoring to inventory keeping of hospitals, every field is using technology and computing. Thus, techniques and methods need to be introduced along with a roadmap to enable inclusion

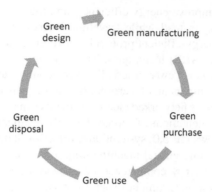

FIGURE 2.2   The process for green practices in healthcare.

of green and sustainable practices. There is a need of a roadmap for this so that hospitals and workers in the healthcare field understand the steps to be taken to make their procedures green and reduce their carbon footprints. The procedure followed by this is illustrated in Figure 2.2. The process for green practices includes the cycle of green design, green manufacturing, green purchase, green use and green disposal. By following this, green practices can be achieved.

Green design practices include hardware as well as software used for healthcare purposes in hospitals and healthcare centers. This includes computers as well as other connecting devices, network devices, storage, etc. Green manufacturing and purchase encompasses healthcare settings to also include data centers. Use of energy-efficient practices and devices also includes making users aware of small steps like switching off systems and enabling sleep mode on computers when not in use, etc. all of which even though small can contribute to the larger picture. Green use involves using green IoT, cloud and other such services. Green disposal includes e-waste and its disposal in a manner so as to reduce environmental impacts. All hospitals should follow proper e-waste disposal protocols and encourage recycling and reuse to reduce environmental hazards.

2.5   CHALLENGES

Companies are now moving towards green IT practices. Dell, Apple and HP are the companies considered as green tech leaders by GreenFactor (a global technology and environmental research initiative). Dell is working to reduce the energy requirements of its data centers and hardware. It is working to reduce hazardous substances in its computer too. Apple claims its notebooks meet the new Energy Star 5.0 specifications and uses mercury-free LED back lighted displays and PVC-free components. The practice of green and sustainable computing in healthcare however faces many challenges. The most common problem faced is by the users. Users are not aware of the existing green technologies. There is a need to enhance the awareness of environmental issues. Awareness about the use of the technology to reduce environmental problems and reduction of carbon emissions should be widespread.

The challenges also include cost, quality and reach: including treatment and operative costs, extending the reach of healthcare services and improving the quality (improve diagnostics and better outcomes from patient treatments) all while maintaining green and sustainable practices [24]. Processing power is vital for business, and its demand is ever increasing with the exponential rise in the number of users. Having environment-friendly practices is limited by the infrastructure limitations. Challenges are faced not only by IT equipment users but also by vendors. Actually, implementing green data centers is a very difficult task due to increase in energy requirements and the increasing energy costs. Equipment life cycle management also becomes difficult for green techniques. Disposal of e-waste is another issue because of lack of techniques and infrastructure for it. Data Science and Big Data analytics are comprehensively used in the healthcare industry because of its complexity. Hospitals and healthcare can contribute to the green direction by combining big data analytics, IoT and cloud computing. e-Waste must be disposed in a proper manner and recycled as part of a sustainability program. Old systems can be replaced by energy-efficient systems. These include virtual servers, virtual data storage, and efficient application and database structures. They can lead to reduced IT power consumption.

Another challenge can be the use of renewable energy. Although they are advised for reduced carbon emission, their setup is costlier than conventional grid energy. Another problem they face is that renewable energy is not reliable and may also face the problem of availability. Another issue is the accuracy of existing energy estimation tools. Examples of such tools include Nokia Energy Profiler, PowerTutor and Trepn Profile. They are used to estimate the energy consumption. They utilize smartphone, and their accuracy is low because of low precision of "fuel gauge sensors used in smartphone batteries." New green technologies like GreenHadoop face difficulties while estimating the energy and time requirements for a job. Scheduling decisions are made on this basis which may suffer. The task of waste heat utilization measures in data centers requires costly thermal heat exchange materials. Green measures adoption may prove to be difficult with cost-efficient business operations. While using cloud computing as a green technology, the main challenge faced is reduction of energy use along with providing quality of service satisfying the requirements. Changes made to the existing systems to incorporate green technology may impact the availability and quality of service. In healthcare applications, availability and quality are very important requirements, which cannot be compromised upon. Quality of service (QoS)-based resource selection and provisioning play a significant role because resource selection and provision can result in energy efficiency [23]. Another problem is of interoperability is that many public cloud systems are not designed for interaction. There is a lack of industry standards to allow the design of interoperable cloud platforms. Energy-aware dynamic resource allocation can also cause issues. The reliability of servers could be affected by their excessive power cycling. Interruption of energy in the cloud environment affects the quality of the provided service. VM migrations used may also lead to high costs for resource consolidation over long-haul networks.

In "big data" for healthcare, challenges include increasing adoption rates for electronic medical records while having environment-friendly infrastructure.

In green IoT, the challenges faced include infrastructure green IoT architectures, spectrum management, communication, security and QoS.

There is an issue of connection between heterogeneous networks, containing different types of devices, running on different platforms and for a variety of applications. Introduction of energy-efficiency in them may be a challenge. Energy-efficient communication protocols deployment for energy efficient communication between IoT should be without compromising the reliability of connectivity. In the fields of security and privacy, algorithms which are energy efficient put the burden of computation on IoT devices. This may in fact cause more energy consumption. Operational costs of systems decrease when adopting green computing practices. Green computing activities allocate IT resources in low system power and idle states which must ensure no reduction in quality of service and availability especially in real time applications. The management of aging and out of date old devices, systems and other resources is a serious activity. Older hardware devices have increased power consumption and require resource replacements and disposals.

The efforts towards green computing are in limited areas and focus on reduced energy consumption and e-waste. The future of green computing will depend on efficiency and green products.

There is a need of government policies that provide incentives to green cloud computing business providers and users. Also estimation is noteworthy in renewable energy technology and power consumption measurement etc. and requires better techniques and research in this area. High estimation accuracy with limited estimation overhead is the requirement. Software operational cost based estimation should be improved for accurate estimation of code storage location. All these are upcoming research areas requiring new and innovative solutions.

2.6   CASE STUDIES

Kooweerup Regional Health Service (KRHS), Australia, has taken steps to introduce practices that make their center green and sustainable. As a part of the GGHH (Global Green and Healthy Hospitals) initiative, their Agenda Goals included energy efficiency and Hospital Goals aimed at reducing energy costs and carbon dioxide emissions [25]. Health services consume high amounts of energy to deliver services to communities. The aim of KRHS is to conserve resources through education, infrastructure, engineering and behavior change. The steps taken by them include use of renewable energy source, i.e., solar energy by having solar tunnels across organization. Light sensors were installed in all clinical storage areas along with review of lighting across the organization. A switch off campaign (SEHCP) was started with stickers on PCs reminding people to switch off lights and shut down computers. They held community workshop and sustainable home program to focus on energy. The benefits obtained by them include financial benefits in the form of unit savings of USD $1922 (AUD$2500) per annum with a return on investment of 4 years. Environmental benefits include saving 28,500 kWh, 100 gigajoules of energy and 38 tons of carbon emissions (tCO$_2$-e).

WHO also is working towards green and sustainable healthcare. Project Optimize between the WHO and PATH was aimed to identify ways to optimize the immunization supply chains to congregate the needs of an increasing, huge and costly portfolio of vaccines. Creation of an ideal vaccine supply chain supporting stronger, more adaptable and more efficient logistics systems was the goal in order to extend the reach of lifesaving health technologies to people around the world [26]. The Cameroon Baptist Convention Health Services (CBCHS) in Cameroon aimed to fulfill the GGHH Agenda Goals of energy efficiency and hospital goals of improved energy access and dependability with clean renewable energy and energy costs reduction. An estimated $2300 US was spent annually on fuel now replaced by solar energy. Savings achieved from the use of renewable energy are now being used for patients through other infrastructural development. Some hospitals replaced security lights with solar panels [26].

A study was carried out to examine the financial and environmental costs associated in the two types of anesthetic equipment. A hospital (Western Health) in Melbourne, Australia, that uses primarily reusable anesthetic equipment was compared with the Austin Hospital in the same city that uses primarily single-use anesthetic equipment. Assessment was made to model the environmental and financial costs of different scenarios. The primary environmental costs considered were CO_2 emissions and water use. The Australian hospital changed its operations from single use to reusable anesthetic equipment. This led to a reduction from USD $55,200 (AUD $69,000) to USD $29,600 (AUD $37,000), i.e., approximately USD $25,600 (AUD $32,000), a 46% reduction [27].

2.7 DISCUSSION AND CONCLUSION

This chapter discussed the applications of various green technologies along with sustainable computing techniques in the field of healthcare. The healthcare industry has been revolutionized by the technological advances. It has led to developments in the form of improved surgical equipment and techniques, remote health and patient monitoring, modern digital equipment, and so on. Ubiquitous computing, IoT, cloud computing and big data all have found applications in the healthcare sector from chronic disorders, health and lifestyle monitoring, treatment adherence, remote patient assistance, to hospital management. All this has helped in healthcare facilities being accessible to a wider range of the population. The topic of green and sustainable computing in healthcare is an essential one with the increased usage of technology in everyday life and computing devices being ubiquitous and smart. In this chapter, the healthcare sector and the various strategies which enable green and sustainable computing for it were discussed. These included green and sustainable computing techniques in the cloud, big data and IoT, and at hardware and software levels. Some of them were techniques to make green cloud data centers, renewable energy resources and waste heat utilization. Methods and plans were discussed, which lead to minimal carbon footprints while applying big data techniques in the numerous amounts of healthcare data collected from individuals and hospitals. In medical IoT environments, energy-efficient methods were discussed. GWSN and GM2MC were some other techniques put forward. At the hardware-level configuration networking (zeroconf), Bonjour Sleep Proxy is one of the methods proposed to have energy-efficient computing. The roadmap presented for healthcare settings was to promote green practices. Case studies enable reader to see how green and sustainable computing methods are being used in the real world by people. Thus, the healthcare sector can also be made digital along with introduction of green and sustainable practices in the computing field.

REFERENCES

1. Mardini, M. T., Iraqi, Y., & Agoulmine, N. (2019). A survey of healthcare monitoring systems for chronically Ill patients and elderly. *Journal of Medical Systems*, *43*(3), 50.
2. Kyriazakos, S., Prasad, R., Mihovska, A., Pnevmatikakis, A., op den Akker, H., Hermens, H., & Grguric, A. (2017). eWALL: An open-source cloud-based eHealth platform for creating home caring environments for older adults living with chronic diseases or frailty. *Wireless Personal Communications*, *97*(2), 1835–1875.
3. Al-khafajiy, M., Baker, T., Chalmers, C., Asim, M., Kolivand, H., Fahim, M., & Waraich, A. (2019). Remote health monitoring of elderly through wearable sensors. *Multimedia Tools and Applications*, 78(17), 24681–24706
4. Ghanavati, S., Abawajy, J. H., Izadi, D., & Alelaiwi, A. A. (2017). Cloud-assisted IoT-based health status monitoring framework. *Cluster Computing*, *20*(2), 1843–1853.
5. Quinde, M., Khan, N., Augusto, J. C., van Wyk, A., & Stewart, J. (2018). Context-aware solutions for asthma condition management: A survey. *Universal Access in the Information Society*, *17*(4), 1–23.
6. Verma, P., & Sood, S. K. (2019). A comprehensive framework for student stress monitoring in fog-cloud IoT environment: M-health perspective. *Medical & Biological Engineering & Computing*, *57*(1), 231–244.
7. Chen, M. Y., Lughofer, E. D., & Polikar, R. (2018). Big Data and Situation-Aware Technology for Smarter Healthcare. *Journal of Medical and Biological Engineering*, *38*, 845–846.
8. Dash, S., Shakyawar, S. K., Sharma, M., & Kaushik, S. (2019). Big data in healthcare: Management, analysis and future prospects. *Journal of Big Data*, *6*(1), 54. https://www.computerworld.com/article/3089073/data-center/cloud-computing-slows-energy-demand-us-says.html. Accessed 2018.
9. Löser, F. (2015). *Strategic Information Systems Management for Environmental Sustainability: Enhancing Firm Competitiveness with Green IS* (Vol. 6). Universitätsverlag der TU Berlin.
10. Ebrahimi, K., Jones, G. F., & Fleischer, A. S. (2014). A review of data center cooling technology, operating conditions and the corresponding low-grade waste heat recovery opportunities. *Renewable & Sustainable Energy Reviews*, *31*, 622–638.
11. Shuja, J., Ahmad, R. W., Gani, A., Ahmed, A. I. A., Siddiqa, A., Nisar, K., & Zomaya, A. Y. (2017). Greening emerging IT technologies: Techniques and practices. *Journal of Internet Services and Applications*, *8*(1), 9.
12. Bhattacherjee, S., Das, R., Khatua, S., & Roy, S. (2019). Energy-efficient migration techniques for cloud environment: A step toward green computing. *The Journal of Supercomputing*, *75*(3), 1–29.
13. Liu, K., Jin, H., Chen, J., Liu, X., Yuan, D., & Yang, Y. (2010). A compromised-time-cost scheduling algorithm in swindew-c for instance-intensive cost-constrained workflows on a cloud computing platform. *The International Journal of High Performance Computing Applications*, *24*(4), 445–456.
14. Lin, C., & Lu, S. (2011). Scheduling scientific workflows elastically for cloud computing. In *2011 IEEE 4th International Conference on Cloud Computing*. Washington, DC, IEEE, pp. 746–747.

15. Selvarani, S., & Sadhasivam, G. S. (2010). Improved cost-based algorithm for task scheduling in cloud computing. In *2010 IEEE International Conference on Computational Intelligence and Computing Research (ICCIC)*, Coimbatore, IEEE, pp. 1–5.
16. Usman, M. J., Ismail, A. S., Abdul-Salaam, G., Chizari, H., Kaiwartya, O., Gital, A. Y., ... Dishing, S. I. (2019). Energy-efficient nature-inspired techniques in cloud computing datacenters. *Telecommunication Systems, 71*(2), 275–302.
17. Goiri, Í., Le, K., Nguyen, T. D., Guitart, J., Torres, J., & Bianchini, R. (2012). GreenHadoop: Leveraging green energy in data-processing frameworks. In *Proceedings of the 7th ACM European Conference on Computer Systems* (EuroSys '12). Association for Computing Machinery (ACM), pp. 57–70.
18. Waas, F. M. (2008). Beyond conventional data warehousing—massively parallel data processing with Greenplum database. *International Workshop on Business Intelligence for the* Real-Time Enterprise. Berlin, Heidelberg, Springer, pp. 89–96.
19. Seah, W. K., Eu, Z. A., & Tan, H. P. (2009). Wireless sensor networks powered by ambient energy harvesting (WSN-HEAP)-survey and challenges. *Wireless Communication, Vehicular Technology, Information Theory and Aerospace & Electronic Systems Technology,* In *2009 1st International Conference on Wireless Communication, Vehicular Technology, Information Theory and Aerospace & Electronic Systems Technology*, Aalborg, pp. 1–5
20. Sodhro, A. H., Sangaiah, A. K., Pirphulal, S., Sekhari, A., & Ouzrout, Y. (2019). Green media-aware medical IoT system. *Multimedia Tools and Applications, 78*(3), 3045–3064.
21. Apple. (2009). Mac OS X v10.6: About Wake on Demand, Setting up Wake on Demand, Setting up a Bonjour Sleep Proxy (Apple Article HT3774). 09–15.
22. Kalange Pooja, R. (2013). Applications of green cloud computing in energy efficiency and environmental sustainability.*IOSR Journal of Computer Engineering (IOSR-JCE)*, 25–33. Second International Conference on Emerging Trends in Engineering (SICETE), ISSN:2278-0661,ISBN:2278-8727.
23. Godbole, N. S., & Lamb, J. (2015). Using data science & big data analytics to make healthcare green. *12th International Conference & Expo on Emerging Technologies for a Smarter World (CEWIT)*. Melville, NY, IEEE, pp. 1–6.
24. Ramsay (2019). Case Studies from GGHH Members, https://www.greenhospitals.net/case-studies-energy, www.kooweeruphospital.com.au, Accessed October 2019.
25. Immunization, Vaccines and Biologicals, World Health Organization (WHO) (2019). https://www.who.int/immunization/programmes_systems/supply_chain/optimize/en/.
26. Promoting Environmentally-Friendly Energy Sources Cameroon Baptist Convention Health Center (CBCHS) (2019). https://www.greenhospitals.net/wp-content/uploads/2019/08/GGHH-Case-Study-Promoting-Environmentally-Friendly-Energy-Sources-Cameroon-Baptist-Convention-Health-Center-CBCHS-.pdf.
27. Lakshmi, V. V. K., Panday, A., Mukherjee, A., & Joshi, B. S. (2012). Green computing platforms for biomedical systems. *Handbook of Green Information and Communication Systems*, Oxford, Elsevier, p. 229.

3 Green Computing and Its Related Technologies

Insha Naz, Sameena Naaz, and Ranjit Biswas
Jamia Hamdard

CONTENTS

3.1 INTRODUCTION

Modern IT systems depend upon a complex blend of people, networks and hardware; hence, green computing must to cover up all of these areas (Thomas, n.d.). Soon after the Energy Star programme was introduced, the term "green computing" also came into existence. Green computing attempts to accomplish improved system performance and economic viability(Sasikala, 2013). Since energy is the greatest resource and carbon footprints are considered the greatest threats to the environment, an effort is required to be taken to reduce both the energy consumption and the carbon footprints(Soomro & Sarwar, 2012). For tackling the environmental impact of IT effectively and making the environment safer and greener, we need to adopt an integrated way that solves the problems and focus on these four G's (Murugesan, 2008):

- *Green use –*
  The focus needs to be put on reducing the energy consumption of computer systems and other devices and trying to use them in a way that's environmentally sound.
- *Green discarding –*
  We need to replenish and use again the old computers and appropriately discard the useless computers and other equipment/devices.
- *Green design –*
  Design the computers and electronic devices in such a manner that is more energy proficient and environmentally suitable.
- *Green manufacturing –*
  Manufacturing of electronic peripherals, computer systems and other devices needs to be done in a way that has the least or no effect on the environment.

Focus needs to be shifted to eco-friendly designs like the use of Energy Star devices which enable the equipment to power down to a lesser amount of electric state when not in use, thus saving the energy. Second, biodegradable and renewable materials should be used instead of toxic materials. Absolute environmental sustainability can be achieved by putting our efforts on these four G's. Due to the increasing costs, high resource consumption and various other issues as discussed earlier, greening IT has become and will persist to be a requisite and not just an option.

3.2   RELATED WORK

After the manufacture of computer in 1948, the world has completely changed. It can be counted in top ten inventions of mankind. Tasks that used to take hours can now be done in fraction of seconds with the help of super computers. But global warming and greenhouse effect is drastically increasing day by day; thus, we need to find the ways that can help to achieving the goal of green and safe environment. Green computing as discussed earlier refers to environmentally liable computing, and it can be anything from power management, proficient algorithms, appropriate utilization of the available resources, energy-efficient display alternative, e-waste recycling, reuse, online data storage to telecommuting. Various green computing approaches such as virtualization and green data centers can help to make the environment greener and safer by reducing the carbon footprints. Green computing mostly deals with reducing, reuse and recycling of IT system like hardware and software application (Pau & Dangwal, 2012).

3.3   GREEN COMPUTING APPROACHES

Some of the approaches used by the organizations towards green computing are discussed next.

3.3.1   POWER MANAGEMENT

The data that was provided by the Intel Labs says that the key part of power utilized by a server is hailed by CPU, then by the memory and eventually by the losses due to power supply inadequacy (Bobby, 2015). Power consumption can be minimized in many effortless yet efficient and effective techniques like using the both sides of the paper for printing, printing only the required pages, reducing the brightness of the screen saving the battery which in turn helps in saving the power, and most importantly turning off the device when not in use. The use of LED and LCD monitors in place of CRTs (Mumbai & Mumbai, 2013) helps in less power consumption. Using the blend of group policies, Windows in-built sleep function and various other third-party software systems such as Tivoli systems, BigFix and EZ GPO can help in power management. Enabling the hibernation mode in system makes the data shift to the hard disk of system initially, and then, the system is turned off, and when the system is switched on, all the files become visible as they were left initially, which also helps in power management. When the system is sent in hibernate mode, battery power can also be minimized. Standby mode is another option to reduce the power consumption, but it's not that efficient because the memory is not shut down. All the approaches for power consumption management are depicted in Figure 3.1. (Naaz et al., 2011) (Figure 3.1).

3.3.2   RESOURCE MANAGEMENT

Resource management involves the purchase of eco-friendly and energy-efficient computer hardware peripherals which are designed and programmed in a way that can expand the equipment lifetime. It also deals with the suppliers who lay the stress on creating the environment-friendly devices, proper packaging and efficient waste management strategies (Sabeel, 2017).

Turn off the computer when not using.
Switch off the External Devices when not needed.
Facilitate energy management.
Use Devices which consume low energy.
Use handheld equipment rather than PC's for basic tasks.

FIGURE 3.1   Approaches for lowering the power consumption.

3.3.3 SERVER VIRTUALIZATION

Virtualization refers to the process of creating two or more logical versions of a single physical hardware. In other words, virtualization can also be referred to as making a lone section of hardware work as numerous different parts. This works by isolating different user interfaces of the hardware, thus making all of them to act and function independently. Virtualization makes proficient use of resources available to the system which results in greater efficiency. Installing virtual infrastructures in data centers permits different operating systems and multiple applications to operate on less servers, which in turn reduces the energy largely used for cooling data center. Server Virtualisation Architecture is described in Figure 3.2. (Patil & Kharade, 2016; Naaz et al., 2012).

Energy saving is the major objective these days; thus, server virtualization is rising as the chief way to merge applications from numerous applications to a single server. In this era of technology, it has been found that virtualization helps in significant energy savings and would be one of the best methodologies to help save tremendous amount of energy, making green computing a sustainable approach for achieving a greener and safer environment with no compromise on technological requirements of current as well as future generations (Motochi et al., 2017).

Virtualization offers the software for virtualization and also the management of the virtual software in virtualized environments. It is a type of green computing which leads to server consolidation, thus enhancing the security of the computer systems. It runs less systems at high level of utilization allowing full utilization of the available resources which results in the decline of entire quantity of hardware used, switching off the inactive virtual server to save available resources and energy as well, and most importantly reduction in the cost by saving the space and rent requirements (Soomro & Sarwar, 2012).

Quite a lot of commercial companies nowadays are offering software packages to smooth the progress of virtual computing. In order to facilitate virtualized computing, Intel Corporation and AMD have also fabricated proprietary

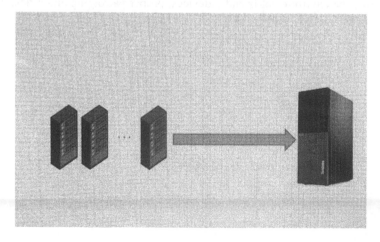

FIGURE 3.2   Server virtualization.

virtualization improvements to the x86 instruction set into each of their CPU product line (Figure 3.2).

3.3.4   The Design of the Data Center

The key issue associated with data centers these days is the escalating economic and environmental costs due to the high energy consumption. Hence, there is dire need for designing of a "green data center" that implies a data center architected in such a way that is energy efficient and releases the minimum amount of CO_2 lowering the overall carbon foot prints (Sabeel, 2017).

The design of the data center is one of the major concerns in modern days; that is, we need to design the data center in such a way that it leaves no or least harmful effects on our environment. According to the figures given, a single Big Data center consumes energy equal to one small city and all the energy consumed doesn't go into cohering the IT equipment. A minimum 50% of the energy is consumed for cooling purpose of IT equipment, the power transmissions and other related overhead(Sharma et al., 2017). And among these, the main power consumption section is the cooling system in data centers which needs to be optimized.

The designing of data center is a significant component to reduce energy consumption. Data center is a place where huge housing of computing, storage and networking devices are stored. And cooling is the chief issue to handle so that the temperature of the data center remains maintained. Big Data centers spend a vast amount of money for electricity consumption every year for cooling purpose at data centers. The data center design can indirectly affect the electricity consumption during cooling process; thus, the better design of data center is the one that consumes lesser amount of energy (Saikumar, 2014).

Few things affecting the decrease in energy consumption in data centers are implementation of basic strategies, centralizing the storage and designing the correct infrastructure/architecture.

In order to run efficiently a data center needs to focus on five vital zones that need to be taken into consideration during designing: the cooling system, conditions of the environment, electrical system, e-waste and system recycling. For handling tremendous quantity of traffic, data center is a key to any organization whether that is big or small. Google is having an efficient data center handling tons of data of every minute. A data center might have a few interconnected servers to numerous interconnected servers depending upon the needs of the organization (Sari & Akkaya, 2015).

According to a survey, IT industry uses almost 3% of the total world's energy. Thus, the management of data center needs to run its operations in an eco-friendly way (Naaz et al., 2010). On the other hand, data centers can take various measures that can minimize the energy consumption such as utilizing renewable energy sources, which are given as follows:

Geothermal energy – Data centers can use geothermal energy which is obtainable naturally in bulk.
Solar energy – Installation of the solar panels is a very familiar and energy efficient way to meet the organization's power needs.

Wind energy – It is another natural source that can be used of now, but till now very less organizations make use of wind turbines as a source of energy

Recycling heat – Many companies are recycling heat that is released from racks reverse for generating energy.

3.3.5   ECO-LABELING OF IT PRODUCT

Eco-labeling basically originated because of the increasing environmental concerns worldwide. Labels like eco-friendly, recyclable, energy efficient and reusable attracted consumers who were basically looking for the ways to diminish the impact of hazardous material on the environment. Eco-labels give the information regarding the existence or nonexistence of particular feature in any product. It enables the customers to get an insight about the environmental quality of items at the time of purchasing, allowing them to pick or buy products that are suitable from an environmental point of view, therefore minimizing the utilization of harmful substances that may be detrimental to the environment.

Companies have to make sure that they manufacture and design products in such a way that they can obtain the eco-label. Many organizations grant certificates to IT products after reviewing the features like energy and resource consumption, recycling and refurbishing, thereby enabling the customers to make the environmentally suitable decision at the time of purchasing a product (Mumbai & Mumbai, 2013) (Figure 3.3).

3.3.6   LIABLE DISPOSAL AND RECYCLING OF e-WASTES

All the broken, out of order, obsolete electronic devices and components are the fastest rising fragment of world's waste stream and has become a global threat. e-Waste is very hazardous to our environment because of the toxic materials present in the electronic devices.

Growing use of technology nowadays has led to the creation of an enormous quantity of electronic wastes resulting in environmental degradation; therefore, the safety of environment and keeping the check on environmental pollution has become the chief concern of scientists all over the world. The main and most important

FIGURE 3.3   EPEAT: the electronic product environmental assessment tool – universal rating system for safer and greener electronics.

concern related to e-wastes is that these are non-biodegradable and their dumping has led to the accretion of toxic materials such as lead and cadmium in the environment resulting in global warming and contamination of the soil and ground water, thereby disturbing the plant and animal life which in turn have an effect on the entire living organisms yielding harsh health risks and disorders. Increasing global warming and mounting energy expenses has led the government as well as the private organizations to think and examine different ways to safeguard the environment worldwide (Panda, 2013).

Enhanced reuse, repair, recycling and discarding of electronic wastes can avoid the e-wastes hazards. Recycling the computing peripherals in an eco-friendly way can keep the dangerous materials such as led, mercury and cadmium away from the landfills. Also the reuse of computing equipment can be done in numerous ways. Different old equipment can be reviewed for figuring out if those equipment enclose various components such as memory and hard drives which can be used to in some other devices for either repairing or upgrading (Singh, 2016).

The most preferred way to tackle the issue of e-wastes is to reduce the usage of electroic devices that means only take what you need, and the least preffered method is recycling.We need to find new ways for using things that are otherwise thrash and try to purchase products that are reusable. E-Waste Manageent process is depicted in Figure 3.4.

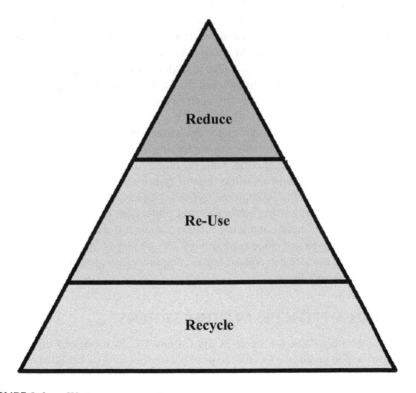

FIGURE 3.4   e-Waste management.

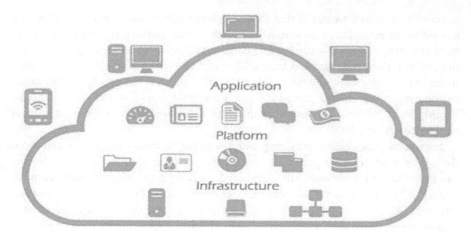

FIGURE 3.5   Architecture of green cloud computing.

3.3.7   GREEN CLOUD COMPUTING

The research carried out by Pike Research demonstrates that "the wide-spread adoption of cloud computing could lead to a potential 38% reduction in worldwide data center energy expenditures by 2020" (Sourabh et al., n.d.). Cloud computing has proved to be a vital and sound means for virtualizing of data centers and servers so that they can be resource as well as energy efficient. Architecture of Green Cloud Computing is explained in Figure 3.5. Due to high consumption of power and energy in IT firms, they produce harmful gases in the environment resulting in global climate changes. As a result, there is a dire need of cloud computing to go green (Patel et al., 2015).

Cloud computing is one of the major paradigms in modern world because of the fact it has dynamic, high-powered computing abilities, with access to intricate applications and data archiving, with no requirement of any extra computing resources. Since cloud computing offers reliability, scalability and high performance at fewer expenses; thus, cloud computing technologies have a diversity of application domains. By offering promising environmental protection, and economic and technological advantages, cloud computing has revolutionized the modern computing. The various technologies of cloud computing such as energy efficiency, reduced carbon footprints and e-waste can convert cloud computing into green cloud computing (Radu, 2017) (Figure 3.5).

3.4   GREEN APPROACHES IN OTHER SECTORS

For environmentally liable and ecologically responsible decisions and lifestyles, we need to pursue the green ways in all the possible sectors such as health and agriculture. Going green helps to guard the environment and sustain its natural resources for both present and future generations.

3.4.1 GREEN HEALTHCARE

Green healthcare means to adapt the practices and techniques in our healthcare which are environmental-friendly. Healthcare is the chief concern of every individual; thus, it is necessary to provide the best and the utmost quality care to patients. But healthcare is also one of the major contributors to waste, even though the enthusiasm for "going green" less considerable information is available to the medical fraternity. The medical community has a huge chance to put into practice the green and efficient ways in healthcare, e.g., in the field of surgery green practices such as operating theatre waste deduction, environmentally preferable purchasing, reusing single-use medical equipment, management of energy consumption and management of pharmaceutical wastes. Using different green practices, public health and sustainability can be improved.

3.4.2 GREEN AGRICULTURE

We need to make farming a sustainable farming, principally, which means using strong modern framework and sustainability concepts to improve agricultural technique. Things such as weed, pest management, organic fertilizers and seeds need to be dealt in a green way. Going green in farming and agriculture is the need of an hour in modern times. Owing to the increasing threat of climate change, the agricultural sector across the globe has been badly affected which in turn affects the global economic state, climatic changes are caused by human practices; thus, we need to look for such practices which will have the minimal effect on the environment. Different techniques need to be used in our agriculture system. "Green care" implies to the use of agricultural farms for boosting mental and physical health of human beings. Farmers definitely need a proper scientific origins for green services, progress of health policies and economical systems that make these services a predictable income (Braastad, 2015).

3.4.3 GREEN INTERNET OF THINGS

A newly trending concept is the Internet of Things (IoT) which connects billions and trillions of devices with each other. Green IoT has abundant number of expertise and research areas enabling universal connectivity over the global physical objects. The four major technologies that enable IoT are radio-frequency identification (RFID), optical tags and quick response codes, Bluetooth low energy (BLE) and wireless sensor network. Green IoT promotes lower power consumption than IoT and makes the environment safer and greener. The life cycle contains green design, manufacturing in green ways, green utilization of available resources and green disposal of the wastes with a negligible impact on the environment (Sadiku et al., 2018).

Due the remarkable development in the field of IoT, the way of working and living has completely changed. Even though the abundant benefits of IoT are improving the society, but IoT also consumes a large amount of energy, leaving toxic pollution and e-waste in the environment. Thus, increasing the benefits of IoT and reducing the harms have become the chief concern. Green IoT is viewed as the future of IoT that is environmentally-friendly. For achieving that, it is compulsory to put a lot of measures to trim down carbon emission rates, consume less resource and persuade proficient techniques for energy usage. The machines, communications, network sensors, clouds and most importantly the internet should be energy efficient and focus on reducing carbon emission rates.

3.4.4 GREEN MARKETING

Selling or marketing the products that are environmentally safe refers to green marketing. Nowadays, the firms and various organizations are using the trend of green as a means for gaining the profit and shielding the environment. To protect the environment and the health of the living beings, the firms and customers have now started to challenge eco-friendly products. Thus, as an element of social sense of right and wrong, the firms have slowly and gradually applied green marketing practices for marketing various products. Since modern day people are way too much concerned about the environment, many firms and industries are using green marketing to amplify their competitive advantages. The companies strictly need to abide by the consumers' requirements. Consumers nowadays are happily eager to pay more money for a better and greener life style. Thus, it can be concluded that green marketing is off course not only the way to make the environment safe but also a smart marketing approach (Fuiyeng& Yazdanifard, 2015).

3.4.5 GREEN ECONOMY

"Green economy or green growth," the latest trend in global environmental governance, was first introduced by a group of top environmental economists in pioneering 1989 report in the United Kingdom, titled *Blueprint for a Green Economy* (UN, 2012).

Green economy is related to ecological economics but has more focus on applied part. It attempts to achieve sustainable development without demeaning the environment. It can be defined as the economy that intends to minimize the environmental threats and ecological insufficiencies. According to UNEP Green Economy Report,

> that to be green, an economy needs to be efficient and fair. Fairness means knowing global as well as the country level equity dimensions, mainly in assuring a just changeover to an economy that is less-carbon, resource proficient, and socially inclusive.

Never (2013)

3.4.6 GREEN INDUSTRY

Green industrial policy or GIP refers to the strategic policy of the government that aims to speed up the growth and development of green industries to shift towards a low-carbon emissions and resource efficiency. A specific challenge faced by GIP is integration of economic and environmental concerns. It also deals with the disinclination of industries to spend in green development.

For improving the poverty issues, creating employments and enhancing the living standards, developing countries require to focus on escalating their industrial sector. But at present, numerous countries are facing severe environmental dilapidation and resource exhaustion, which threaten the chances of sustainable economic growth. Green industry not only encourages the sustainable patterns of production as well as consumption but also provides model that are resource and energy proficient and non-polluting and safe, and release low-carbon emissions and wastes. Green industry plan wraps the greening of industries. The greening of industries also contributes to poverty lessening, promoting energy security, health and safety, jobs, and reducing costs through increased productivity.

3.4.7 GREEN ARCHITECTURE

Sustainability is the common interest of numerous disciplines in modern times. The concept of green architecture or sustainable architecture refers to constructing building in such a way that reduces the hazardous effects of construction on human health and the environment. The "green" architect tries to maintain the air and water quality by selecting eco-friendly construction materials and practices.

Green architecture means environment-friendly architecture having various characteristics such as

1. Energy-efficient lighting and appliances
2. A ventilation system planned and designed for proficient heating and cooling
3. Water-saving fixtures
4. Minimal or no damage to the natural habitat
5. Alternate power sources
6. Non-toxic materials
7. Efficient use of space.

Green architecture has environmental, social as well as economic benefits. It helps in one of the major concerns of modern times that is pollution reduction and promotes natural resources conservation, and also reduces the amount of money that has to be used on water and energy, and green buildings are meant to be striking and beautiful, thus causing only negligible sprain on the local infrastructure (Ragheb et al., 2016).

3.5 CHALLENGES IN GOING GREEN

Some problems can arise in going green. Few challenges faced in going green are discussed next.

3.5.1 LIFE STYLE PROBLEMS AND ISSUES

Nowadays, everybody is so addicted to technology that all our daily life jobs revolve around electronics, which is almost impossible to get compromised easily.

3.5.2   People Don't Dump e-Wastes Appropriately

e-Waste, the major concern of the modern times needs to be dumped in proper way. Biodegradable and non-biodegradable waste needs to dumped separately; there should be a proper waste dumping system.

3.5.3   Poor Accessibility of Eco-friendly Products

Eco-friendly products are not readily available and are very costly.

3.5.4   Lack of Awareness among the General Masses

People are not fully aware of all the right and wrong things that concern the environment, and even if someone tries to educate, people are not ready to learn.

3.5.5   Planting Trees Is a Challenge

It gets difficult to plant trees because of the insufficiency of land due to increasing population.

3.6   CONCLUSION

From the study of various green technologies and their uses, it can be concluded that going green is the need of hour in modern times. Due to the increasing use of IT nowadays our environment is degrading very fast; thus, different ways need to be used to make our environment greener and safer, and we should be able to sustain the natural resources for present as well as future generations. Various sectors such as healthcare, agriculture and marketing are going green so that there is minimal or no harmful effect on the environment. Focus needs to be shifted to areas where there is dire need to achieve greening.

REFERENCES

Bobby, S. (2015). Green Computing Techniques to Power Management and Energy Efficiency, (March), *3*(6), 107–112.

Braastad, B. O. (2015). COST Action 866 : Green Care in Agriculture Bjarne O. Braastad (Chairman).

Fuiyeng, W., & Yazdanifard, R. (2015). Green Marketing: A Study of Consumers' Buying Behavior in Relation to Green Products, *15*(5).

Motochi, V., Barasa, S., Owoche, P., & Wabwoba, F. (2017). The Role of Virtualization Towards Green Computing and Environmental Sustainability, *6*(6), 851–858.

Mumbai, N., & Mumbai, N. (2013). Green Computing : An Essential Trend for Secure, (April), V-19 P–20.

Murugesan, S. (2008). Harnessing Green IT : Principles and Practices - Adopting a Holistic Approach to Greening IT is our Responsibility toward Creating a More Sustaining Environment, (February), 24–33. https://doi.org/10.1002/9781118305393

Naaz, S., Alam, A., & Biswas, R. (2010). Implementation of a New Fuzzy Based Load Balancing Algorithm for Hypercubes, 270–274.

Naaz, S., Alam, A., & Biswas, R. (2011). Effect of Different Defuzzification Methods in a Fuzzy Based Load Balancing Application, *8*(5), 261–267.

Naaz, S., Alam, A., & Biswas, R. (2012). Load Balancing Algorithms for Peer to Peer and Client Server Distributed Environments, *47*(8), 17–21. https://doi.org/10.5120/7208–9995.

Nations, U. (n.d.). Policies for supporting Green Industry.

Never, B. (2013). GIGA Research Programme : Assessing Countries ' Green Power Toward the Green Economy : Babette Never, 226.

Panda, R. (2013). E-waste Management : A Step Towards, *4*(5), 417–424.

Patel, Y. S., Mehrotra, N., & Soner, S. (2015). Green Cloud Computing : A Review on Green IT Areas for Cloud Computing Environment, 327–332.

Patil, P. S., & Kharade, J. (2016). A Study on Green Cloud Computing, 11141–11148. https://doi.org/10.15680/IJIRCCE.2016.

Pau, P. K., & Dangwal, K. L. (2012). Green Computing : Opportunities and Problems in the Perspective of Developing Countries, *1*(2).

Pazowski, P. (n.d.). Green Computing : Latest Practices and Technologies for ICT Sustainability Computing Approaches, 1853–1860.

Radu, L. (2017). SS symmetry Green Cloud Computing : A Literature Survey. https://doi.org/10.3390/sym9120295.

Ragheb, A., El-shimy, H., & Ragheb, G. (2016). Green Architecture : A Concept of Sustainability, *216*, 778–787. https://doi.org/10.1016/j.sbspro.2015.12.075.

Sabeel, U. (2017). Green Computing-An Environmentally Sustainable Modus Operandi, *7*(5), 192–196. https://doi.org/10.23956/ijarcsse/SV7I5/0192.

Sadiku, M. N. O., Nelatury, S. R., & Musa, S. M. (2018). Available online www.jsaer.com Review Article Green IOT : A Primer, *5*(10), 49–52.

Saikumar, K. (2014). Design of Data Center, *2*(6), 147–149.

Sari, A., & Akkaya, M. (2015). Security and Optimization Challenges of Green Data Centers, (December), 492–500.

Sasikala, P. (2013). Research Challenges and Potential Green Technological Applications in Cloud Computing, *2*(1), 1–19.

Sharma, P., Ii, P. P., Irwin, D., & Goodhue, J. (2017). Design and Operational Analysis of a Green Data Center.

Singh, S. (2016). Green computing strategies & challenges. *Proceedings of the 2015 International Conference on Green Computing and Internet of Things, ICGCIoT 2015*, (1), 758–760. https://doi.org/10.1109/ICGCIoT.2015.7380564.

Soomro, T. R., & Sarwar, M. (2012). Green Computing : From Current to Future Trends, *6*(3), 326–329.

Sourabh, K., Aqib, S. M., & Elahi, A. (n.d.). Sustainable Green Computing : Objectives and Approaches, 672–681.

Thomas, R. (n.d.). Approaches in Green Computing.

UN. (2012). A guidebook to the Green Economy Issue 1: Green Economy, Green Growth, and Low-Carbon Development – history, definitions and a guide to recent publications Division for Sustainable Development, UNDESA, (1).

4 Wearable Computing and Its Applications
An Approach towards Sustainable Living

Aqeel Khalique, Imran Hussain, Zeeshan A. Haq, Tabrej A. Khan, and Safdar Tanweer

Jamia Hamdard

CONTENTS

4.1   INTRODUCTION

Wearable computing is defined as computing performed by the devices worn by humans. It is, generally, performed to determine analytical results pertaining to the person wearing these devices. Thus, wearable devices allow their user to work, communicate ,and provide infotainment at the same time ensuring mobility and hand-free or eye-free access to the device. Wearable computing is fusing with fashion industry as the market is very versatile and the major target segment is consumers of all age group, genders etc. Wearable market is growing rapidly with a statistics of 27.9 million units sold in Q2 of 2018 [1]. Major market players include Apple, Google, Xiaomi, and Huawei. Many other big companies are also investing in wearable industry due to the versatile nature of the industry. Figure 4.1 shows a generalized portfolio of the wearable devices that include smart watches, smart shoes, smart clothing, and hearing aids [2]. These devices are majorly classified in several

FIGURE 4.1   Product portfolio of wearable devices.

FIGURE 4.2   Consumer areas of wearable devices.

application domains including healthcare and medical services, fitness and wellness services, infotainment services, and military and industrial services as shown in Figure 4.2. According to a statistic, wearable market presently is more than $5 billion today and is expecting to reach $50 billion in next 5 years [3].

Wearable devices lack clear specification and standards as per the industry norms because of the emerging nature and evolving technologies in the development of wearable devices. In this chapter, we concisely present the important features of wearable devices. These features are listed as follows:

- Embedded processing unit in the wearable device.
- Continuous communication between user and device.
- Interrupt-free data collection and computation of real-time data.
- More personalized for the user as it is worn on the body by the user.

Tesla Inc. has drafted present requirements for a device to be called as wearable device [4]. These requirements are listed as follows:

- $R1$ – It should be easily wearable for a longer period of time.
- $R2$– It should be smart in design having advanced circuitry, seamless wireless connectivity, and self-sufficient processing potential.
- $R3$ – It should give uninterrupted and constant access to information services with user interruptions as required.
- $R4$ – It should sense user's internal state and provide the best subjective support.
- $R5$ – It should not distract user during normal operation.
- $R6$ – It should ensure privacy and personal information must be kept confidential.
- $R7$ –It should be personalized according to the user's preferences, taste, habits etc.
- $R8$ – It should provide a medium to the user (interface) for computation of the desired output based on the user's preference and device abilities.

Wearable devices operate in ubiquitous environment and perform communication for all the connected devices in the environment. The ubiquitous nature of these devices extends the scope of functionalities and application usability as the need of the user in the given environment. Therefore, here, we accumulate the features and requirements for a device to be called as a wearable device and, hence, present distinct attributes which make a computing device as wearable device. These attributes are listed as follows:

- Device is distraction free with hand-free operation including voice and gesture control capabilities.
- Continuous operation, i.e., always switched on.
- Sense data from environment through sensors including GPS, accelerometer, compass, microphone, and camera.
- Always connected using enabling communication technologies such as Wi-Fi, Bluetooth, and NFC.

However, wearable devices have been evolved in huge manner. In last 10 years, wearable devices have advanced in two primary areas:

- Ability to collect personal data
- Ability to perform real time data insights to the users

Based on the usability and scope of technology, major market players have come forward into wearable industry for development of wearable devices. The increase in the development of wearable devices by numerous big giants is primarily due to increased usability in these consumer areas as shown in Figure 4.2. The increase in usability and technological advancement give birth to another concern of sustainability. This chapter will discuss in detail the sustainability options of these devices and the effect of the usability and technological advancement of these devices onto the users' well-being, i.e., sustainable living.

4.2 HISTORY AND EVOLUTION OF WEARABLE DEVICES

Wearable devices were first introduced half a century ago. There are numerous recorded and published literatures regarding the history of wearable devices. Table 4.1 shows remarkable work related to wearable devices in chronological order; however, the list presented is not exhaustive:

With the evolution in technology, wearable devices also evolved from wrist worn watches to smart watches capable of numerous functionalities. Figure 4.3 shows chronological timeline with the advancement in wearable devices.

TABLE 4.1
Remarkable Work Related to Wearable Devices in Chronological Order

Year	Major Contribution
1961	Edward O. Thorpe invented basic wearable computer to predict winning roulette [5]. The device was a small-sized analog computing device with four push buttons. There is a datataker which can use the buttons to show the speed of the roulette wheel and the device sends tones over radio to a person's hearing aid.
1967	Hubert Upton invented a computer mounted within a pair of eyeglasses to assist hearing-impaired individuals by lip reading [6].
1977	CC Collins developed wearable camera-to-tactile vest for the blind [7]. The device was a five-pound wearable with a head-mounted camera that can convert images in a square tactile grid on a vest.
1978	Eudaemonic Enterprises invented a digital wearable computer in a shoe to predict roulette wheels using a CMOS 6502 microprocessor with 5K RAM. The device was a shoe computer with toe-control and inductive radio communications with between a data taker and better [8].
1979	Sony introduced the Walkman, a commercial wearable cassette player [9]. Sony Founder and Chief Advisor, Masaru Ibuka and Akio Morita, created the concept of the Walkman portable stereo for enjoying personal music while walking.

(Continued)

TABLE 4.1 (*Continued*)
Remarkable Work Related to Wearable Devices in Chronological Order

Year	Major Contribution
1981	Steve Mann designed a backpack-mounted computer to control cameras and other photographic equipment [10]. The backpack-mounted device had a 6502 computer into a steel-frame backpack to control flash-bulbs, cameras, and other photographic systems. The display was a camera viewfinder CRT attached to a helmet. The device was powered by lead-acid batteries.
1991	Carnegie Mellon's Engineering Design Research Center at CMU developed VuMan 1 [11] for viewing house blueprints. Input was taken from a three-button unit worn on the belt, and output was generated over Reflection Tech's Private Eye. The CPU was an 8 MHz 80188 processor with 0.5 MB ROM.
1993	BBN invented a Pathfinder system consisting of a wearable computer with GPS and radiation detection system [10].
1994	Mik Lamming and Mike Flynn developed [12]. "Forget-Me-Not," a continuous personal recording system .The wearable device could store interactions with people and devices, and update this information in a database for data processing.
1994	Edgar Matias developed a "wrist computer" with half-QWERTY keyboard. The device had a modified HP 95LX palmtop computer and a half-QWERTY one-handed keyboard [13].
1994	DARPA introduced Smart Modules Program to develop a modular, human-wearable computers (A brief history of wearable computing). The device had radios, navigation systems, human–computer interfaces, etc. for military and commercial use.
1994	Steve Mann developed "Wearable Wireless Webcam" for transmitting images from a head-mounted analog camera to base station [14]. The images were processed by the base station and displayed on a webpage in near realtime.
2001	Wearable computers used for video conferencing using a digital broadband network [15].
2006	System for Wearable Audio Navigation (SWAN) was a wearable system to enhance audio navigation for the visually impaired [16].
2013	Google Glass is an optical head mounted display like eyewear. It has a touchpad on side of eyewear, a camera, and a display on eyeglasses.
2014	Apple Watch uses a wireless connection with an iPhone. It has several functions and voice automated Siri to assist user's voice commands.

FIGURE 4.3   Technological evolution of wearable devices chronologically.

4.3   INDUSTRIAL GROWTH AND WEARABLE PORTFOLIO

As shown in Figure 4.4, a report by Berkeley shows the cumulative wearable devices being shipped in the world market. These devices include smart watches, smart glasses, smart clothing, fitness trackers, body sensors, wearable cameras, and other wearable devices [17].

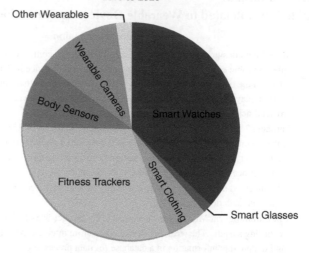

FIGURE 4.4 Graph depicting cumulative sales of wearable devices across the globe from 2013 to 2020.

Wearable devices offer functionality in the abovementioned domains. The functions which are performed by the wearable devices are numerous although important functionalities are shown in Figure 4.5.

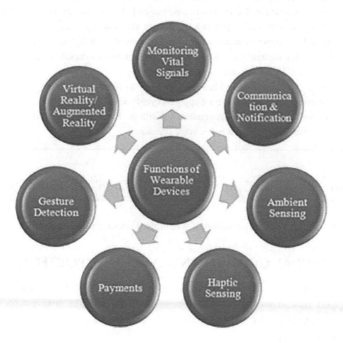

FIGURE 4.5 Functions of wearable devices.

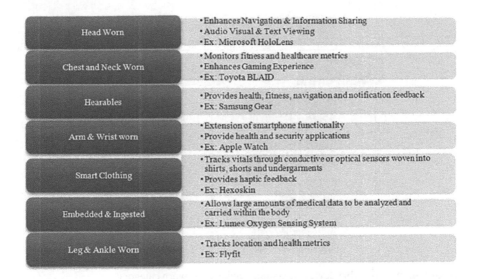

Head Worn	• Enhances Navigation & Information Sharing • Audio Visual & Text Viewing • Ex: Microsoft HoloLens
Chest and Neck Worn	• Monitors fitness and healthcare metrics • Enhances Gaming Experience • Ex: Toyota BLAID
Hearables	• Provides health, fitness, navigation and notification feedback • Ex: Samsung Gear
Arm & Wrist worn	• Extension of smartphone functionality • Provide health and security applications • Ex: Apple Watch
Smart Clothing	• Tracks vitals through conductive or optical sensors woven into shirts, shorts and undergarments • Provides haptic feedback • Ex: Hexoskin
Embedded & Ingested	• Allows large amounts of medical data to be analyzed and carried within the body • Ex: Lumee Oxygen Sensing System
Leg & Ankle Worn	• Tracks location and health metrics • Ex: Flyfit

FIGURE 4.6   Functions provided by wearable devices under different categories.

Wearable devices are categorized by where they are worn on the body of user. Figure 4.5 shows the functionalities of different wearable devices based on where they are worn on the body. Figure 4.6 presents a detailed taxonomy of wearable devices under major categories such as wrist worns, head mounted, e-textiles, and e-patches. In this chapter, we have done an extensive study about different wearable devices and categorized them according to their usability and where they are worn on the user's body. This detailed categorization is presented in the taxonomical structure shown in Figure 4.7, i.e., different parts where these main categories are elaborated to list down wearable devices available in the consumer market globally.

4.4   SUSTAINABLE LIVING: IMPACT OF WEARABLE DEVICES

Nowadays, wearable devices have become a prominent part in human lives. These devices are often called as extended part of human body. Applications of wearable devices have a positive impact on the improvement of quality of life with a value of sustainability. However, wearable devices are continuously evolving influencing

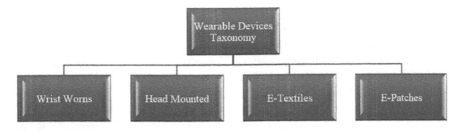

FIGURE 4.7a   Wearable devices taxonomy.

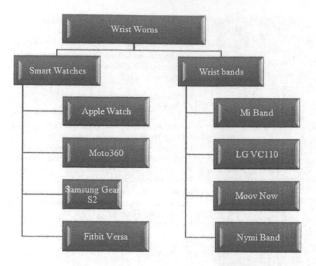

FIGURE 4.7b Wearable devices taxonomy under wrist worn category.

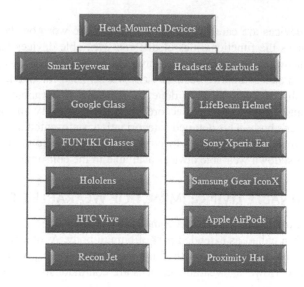

FIGURE 4.7c Wearable devices taxonomy under head mounted category.

human lives and environment. Wearable devices will evolve from collecting simple physical activities or biometric data to improve the quality of life and influence all aspects of human life. Therefore, sustainability plays a vital role in the evolution and growth of wearable devices due to numerous reasons. First, wearable devices must be socially acceptable by the humans. Second, wearable devices must be economically feasible in terms of production and consumption. Lastly, but not least, wearable devices must not pose adverse effects on our environment. Therefore, we can diversify the sustainability aspects of wearable devices in three categories: social

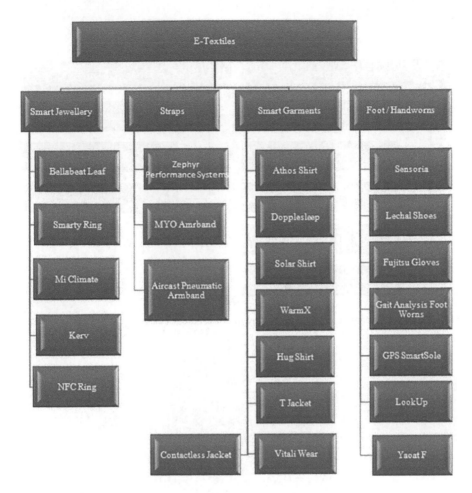

FIGURE 4.7d   Wearable devices taxonomy under e-textile category.

(consisting of humans, consumers, etc.), economic (consisting of production feasibility and consumption affordability), and environmental (consisting of our ecosystem). Figure 4.8 shows the convergence of these three sustainability aspects for wearable devices.

4.4.1   Sustaining Quality of Life

Wearable devices play an important role in sustaining quality of life. As shown in Figure 4.8, convergence of all three aspects of sustainability must be performed in order to improve quality of life, preserving ecosystem and economic development of all sectors of human lives. However, there are sustainability challenges in the path of this convergence. These challenges must be addressed and resolved considering the sustainability aspects and their convergence for improving quality of human lives. The sustainability challenges of wearable devices may include

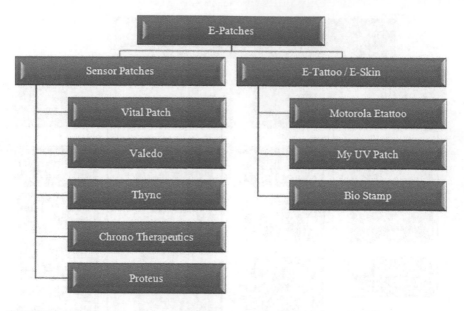

FIGURE 4.7e   Wearable devices taxonomy under e-patches category.

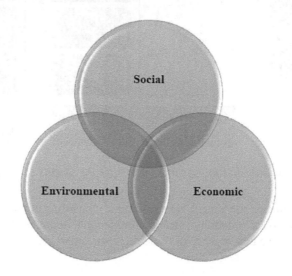

FIGURE 4.8   Convergence of sustainability aspects for wearable devices.

- Technological fusion of ICT and other industries is complicated.
- Short lifespan of consumer goods.
- Frequently changing consumer tastes and preferences.
- Shorter service life and innovation stage.
- Software incompatibility.
- Increased dependency of human lives on these wearable devices.
- Mass production results in resource scarcity and price growth.

- Inadequate recycling process creating difficulty in e-waste management.
- Social acceptance is complicated due to privacy issues.
- Cultural differences across the globe.
- Security of plenty of data may pose new threats coming every day.
- Users' changing needs and requirements.

4.4.2 SUSTAINABLE LIVING: A USER CENTRIC APPROACH

Based on the sustainability aspects of wearable devices as shown in Figure 4.8, the challenges mentioned above can be resolved to an extent. However, wearable devices can have a disruptive influence on current consumption trend. Consumption of new products becomes less by increasing the product lifespan. To achieve increased product lifespan, durable materials should be used, and awareness of knowledge for correct maintenance and cleaning practices should be brought to focus. This approach also helps in e-waste management. As quoted by –Kristi Kuusk (2016), "When an already existing product removes the need to buy a new one, the biggest sustainability benefit to the environment is realized" [18].

Another challenge is user's changing desires and requirements. An alternative solution is to produce adaptable and multi-functional products that can be changed and modified according to the circumstances, usage, and user preferences. For example, color, shape, and temperature-changing materials with self-maintenance functions should be introduced to meet the dynamic requirements of the user. The approach to resolve this challenge is to enhance the emotional attachment between the user and wearable device. By increasing the emotional attachment to a specific device, it is expected to have a longer lifetime. However, this is more complicated to comply. To achieve a stronger attachment, the device has to integrate with the personal taste of the users such as user's values, lifestyle, identity construction, personal memories, and aesthetic requirements. A higher degree of personalization or customization is required to increase the user's emotional attachment. This approach is most suitable in increasing sustainability of wearable devices. The importance of increased emotional attachment between the user and wearable device is listed as follows:

- Increased quality of human life.
- User centric sustainability of wearable devices.
- Emotional attachment brings more ownership and personal belongingness.
- Need of unwanted product purchase by the users will reduce, hence improving e-waste management.
- Retention of wearable devices from one generation to another can preserve cultural heritage.

Lastly, sustainability effects of wearable devices are based on user behavior and interaction of user with the device. Despite the highest sustainability standards and design modifications of the devices, it is the users' dynamic preferences or decisions that can counter these effects. With personalized product designs, many drawbacks can be avoided; however, the resulting user behavior can never be fully controlled.

4.5   SECURITY CONCERNS AND TECHNOLOGICAL CHALLENGES

There are several complications faced by the enterprises including security concerns and legal implications while deploying wearable devices across the globe for mass consumption [19]. Figure 4.9 shows these complications. Technological barriers may limit mass adoption until there are improvements in usage, design, and cost. Figure 4.10 shows these technological barriers.

4.6   CONCLUSION

Wearable devices are becoming cheaper, smarter, and more ubiquitous in nature. Applications of wearable devices vary from smart clothing to military clothing, professional sportswear, and gadgets for determining cognitive intelligence with interdisciplinary collaboration between researchers from different fields. Wearable computing devices are becoming more powerful and growing exponentially because of proliferation of IoT devices and ICT. Wearable devices are being used and worn on body such as smart watch, apparels, and glasses. These wearable devices are used in diversified application areas such as healthcare and medical, fitness and wellness, military, infotainment, retail and logistics, and communications.

In this chapter, we have stated requirements need to be fulfilled by a smart device to be considered as wearable device. We have discussed history and evolution of wearable devices. Wearable devices evolved from small digital watch to smart watch monitoring health-related information. Wearable devices offer functionalities which are very important for users. We have further categorized wearable devices based on where they are worn and listed products falling in these categories.

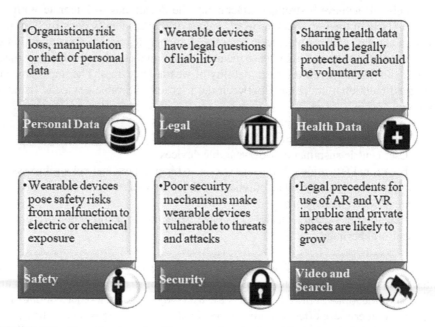

FIGURE 4.9   Complications faced by enterprises in wearable devices industry.

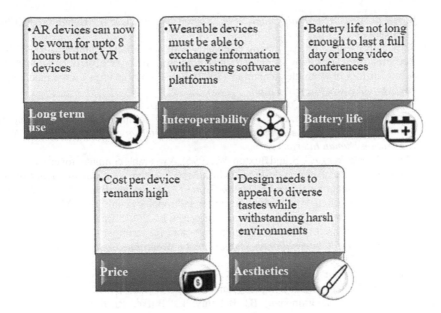

FIGURE 4.10   Technological barriers in wearable devices industry.

With ever-growing use and penetration in human lives, these wearable devices are producing several challenges to the sustainability aspects. These challenges are discussed, and we bring a concept of sustainable living based on user centric approach. The dependency of users on wearable devices may lead to challenges discussed. Therefore, enhancement of human life sustainability can be enhanced by increasing the degree of personalization and emotional attachment between user and wearable device.

REFERENCES

1. Worldwide Wearables Market Ticks Up 5.5% Due to Emerging Markets, Says IDC. (2018, September 04). Retrieved June 02, 2020, from https://www.businesswire.com/news/home/20180904005112/en/Worldwide-Wearables-Market-Ticks-5.5-Due-Emerging
2. Kurzweil accelerating intelligence. (2013). Retrieved from https://www.kurzweilai.net/the-world-of-wearable-computers.
3. Gartner Says Worldwide Wearable Device Sales to Grow 26 Percent in 2019 #GartnerTGI. (2018.). Retrieved from https://www.gartner.com/en/newsroom/press-releases/2018-11-29-gartner-says-worldwide-wearable-device-sales-to-grow-
4. Mikhalchuk, D. (2019). What is wearable computer: Simple guide to the technology. Retrieved from https://teslasuit.io/blog/what-is-wearable-computer-simple-guide/.
5. Thorp, E. O. (1998). The invention of the first wearable computer. Digest of Papers. *Second International Symposium on Wearable Computers* (Cat. No.98EX215), 4–8. doi: 10.1109/iswc.1998.729523.
6. Upton, H.W. (1968). Wearable eyeglass speechreading aid. *American Annals of the Deaf*, 1132, 222–229.
7. Collins, C.C., Scadden, L.A. and Alden, A.B. (1977). Mobile studies with a tactile imaging device. *Fourth Conference on Systems & Devices for the Disabled.*

8. Bass, T. A. (1985). *Eudaemonic Pie.* Boston, Massachusetts: Houghton Mifflin Company.
9. Sony global - press release - Sony celebrates Walkman(R) 20th anniversary. (1999.). Retrieved from https://www.sony.net/SonyInfo/News/Press_Archive/199907/99-059/.
10. A brief history of wearable computing. (2002). Retrieved from https://www.media.mit.edu/wearables/lizzy/timeline.html.
11. Wearable technologies: Concepts, methodologies, tools, and applications. (2018)
12. Lamming, M. and Flynn, M. (1994). "Forget-me-not" intimate computing in support of human memory. *Proceedings of FRIEND21, 94 International Symposium on Next Generation Human Interface.*
13. Matias, E., Mackenzie, I. S. and Buxton, W. (1996). A wearable computer for use in micro-gravity space and other non-desktop environments. *Conference Companion on Human Factors in Computing Systems Common Ground - CHI 96.*doi:10.1145/257089.257146.
14. Mann, S. (2010). Retrieved from http://cyborganthropology.com/Steve_Mann.
15. Hestnes, B., Heiestad, S., Brooks, P. and Drageset, L. (2001). Real situations of wearable computers used for video conferencing - and for terminal and network design. *Proceedings Fifth International Symposium on Wearable Computers.*doi: 10.1109/iswc.2001.962103.
16. SWAN: System for Wearable Audio Navigation. (2003). Retrieved from http://sonify.psych.gatech.edu/research/SWAN/#_blank.
17. Hanuska, A., Chandramohan, B., Bellamy, L., Burke, P., Ramanathan, R. and Balakrishnan, V. (2013). *Smart Clothing Market Analysis.* Berkeley, CA: University of California. Retrieved from http://scet.berkeley.edu/wp-content/uploads/Smart-Clothing-Market-Analysis-Presentation.pdf
18. Vaajakari, J. (2018). How sustainable is wearable technology? Retrieved from https://medium.com/datadriveninvestor/how-sustainable-is-wearable-technology-88608a932cb4.
19. Opher, A., Mehr, H., Onda, A. and Cooper, B. (2017). Leveraging wearables and the Internet of Things to disrupt, transform, and unlock value.*IBM Market Development & Insights.*

5 Role of IoT and Sensors in Achieving Sustainability

Deepak Kumar Sharma,
Shikha Brahmachari, and Ishaan Srivastav
Netaji Subhas University of Technology

CONTENTS

5.1   INTRODUCTION

Internet of Things (IoT) is an uprising technology aiming at connecting various devices. It has redefined the very concept of device connectivity by expanding its role past classic gadgets to non-internet-enabled devices and everyday objects. With prime advantages of IoT, it also faces the challenge of excessive energy consumption by its devices. Deployment of IoT devices and sensors plays a crucial role in achieving environmental sustainability, thereby reducing the detrimental effect on the environment. This chapter first explains the technologies involved with IoT and their deployment for reducing energy expenditure and the overall carbon footprint. It then examines the environmental challenges associated with IoT and the shift towards green IoT to [1] address it. IoT applications are described in brief. It concludes with suggestions for future research and advancements.

5.1.1 TECHNOLOGIES INVOLVED WITH IoT

IoT has the capability of constructing an energy-efficient industrial system and environmental sustainable applications with the help of the technologies associated with it [4]. IoT technologies such as WSN, RFID, edge and cloud computing are used for monitoring and ensuring high performance of the industrial IoT standards with energy-efficient applications [2].

1. *Radio frequency identification system (RFID)* – RFID is an automatic identification system consisting as shown in Figure 5.1 of readers (transmitters/receivers) and tags (transmitters/ responders). There exist six major classifications of RFID tags (0–5). For the identification of an object, it is attached with a tag, which is a microchip in connection with an antenna [3]. Radio waves/frequencies are utilized by RFID tags for communicating with RFID readers [4]. RFID readers are in connection with the terminal of the internet, enabling readers to recognize, monitor, and locate the objects, in real time, automatically, and globally. The automated identification and capturing [5] of data are the major advantages of RFID technology that has brought a significant change in a world of business models and further aims at the reduction of the cost of pre-existing systems like barcodes [17].
2. *Wireless sensor networks (WSNs)* – The components of the WSN consist of gateway nodes and sensors. There are several units for enabling communication and sensing contained by sensor nodes. The deployment of sensor nodes is being carried out for the measurement of global and local

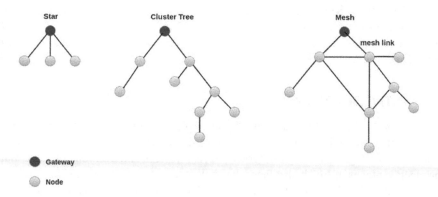

FIGURE 5.1   Components of RFID system.

environmental conditions involving pollution, temperature rise, and climate change. Utilizing the ad-hoc technology, sensors communicate amongst each other and the necessary sensory data is delivered to the gateway. Sensor nodes have small storage capacity along with low processing and limited power, whereas gateway nodes are authoritative in nature [6].

The aim of the microprocessors present in the sensors is to minimize energy consumption and to maximize the speed of the processor. The prime objective of WSN is the enhancement of the environmental system through supplying sufficient energy and provision of valid transmission with reassurance of quality of service (QoS). Figure 5.2 depicts the WSN [7].

3. *Cloud computing* – Cloud computing allows unlimited storage, computational resources, and service delivery over the internet. This is considered to be one of the most efficient models responsible for providing rapid on demand access to shared resources like servers or storage while requiring minimal service provider interaction and management. It is the backend solution for the management of large data streams. There is a provision of scalable, virtual, flexible, and efficient data centres to ensure context-aware computation and online service for the implementation of IoT. Cloud facilitates data collection and its processing required for numerous IoT applications. It also ensures integration of new things and rapid setup, while maintenance cost for deployment is kept low. It is the most cost-effective and convenient solution to [8] deal with the storage issues created due to the data produced by IoT, and thus, there are new opportunities generated for integration, data aggregation, and sharing with third parties Cloud works as a well-defined ecosystem with well-defined Application Programming Interfaces (APIs), top-level security and universal accessibility since data can be directly accessed from anywhere.

4. *Edge computing* – Edge computing allows the computation to be downstream and upstream data based on cloud services and IoT services, respectively, at the network edge [9]. Edge is termed as any type of network resources and computing along the channel between data sources and cloud data centres. Edge computing has certain attributes such as proximity, location tracking, low latency, and geographical distribution. The motive behind this technology is to ensure that computation should be carried out

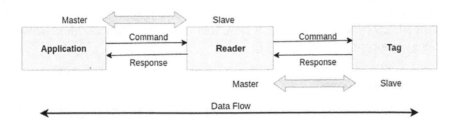

FIGURE 5.2 Wireless sensor networks (WSNs).

in proximity to sources of data. The functions performed by edge computing involve storage of data, service delivery, and request distribution from cloud to user, processing, and caching.

5.2 COMMUNICATION PROTOCOLS

This section primarily focuses on various communication protocols [10] of IoT. These protocols are used for connecting various IoT devices while establishing communication amongst them [11].

5.2.1 NEAR-FIELD COMMUNICATION

Near-field communication (NFC) belongs to the category of short-range wireless communication enabling transmission of data amongst devices by ensuring the devices are only a few inches apart. It establishes bidirectional transmission of data between devices equipped with NFC.NFC contains a tag consisting of a significant amount of data. This tag is only readable or rewritable, and changes can be made using a specific device. NFC operates in three communication modes: passive, active, and peer-to-peer mode. It supports peer-to-peer network topology. NFC works efficiently to connect, maintain, and control IoT devices installed in smart cities, medical and healthcare, workplace, etc. Smart phones integrated with RFID [12] readers make NFC customer-oriented; 13.56 MHz is the frequency band within which the NFC operates. Duration of bits is dependent on the mode of communication, the data transmission rate, and a divisor which exists for a particular mode and transmission rate.

The relation of bit duration is given by [13] the following equation:

$$b_d = (128/D \cdot f_c)S \tag{5.1}$$

where b is the bit duration, f is the carrier frequency, D is the divisor, and S is the communication mode.

5.2.2 Z-WAVE

Z-wave is a low power consumption and wireless MAC protocol supporting mesh network topology. It establishes connection and communication amongst 30–50 nodes, and uses sigma chips in its hardware. It is more suitable for smaller data packets with relatively low speed up to 100 kbps and point-to-point communication within 30 m. Z-wave is composed of slave and controlling devices. Mesh network topology is supported by Z-wave [14].

5.2.3 LTE-ADVANCED

Third-generation cell phones are complex and have a limited capacity, which led to the initiation of long-term evolution (LTE). LTE supports features such as low latency and high data rate. Upgradation of LTE to cope up data traffic, new applications, etc.

leads to the development of LTE-Advanced. LTE-Advanced ensures the provision of different services and applications that are IP (Internet Protocol)-based along with a wide range of transmission rate, various QoS requirements, and mobility conditions. The data rate in LTE-Advanced has been enhanced up to 3Gbps and 1.5Gbps. Carrier aggregation (CA) is the prime facility provided by LTE-Advanced [15]. Both time division duplex (TDD) and frequency division duplex (FDD) are supported by LTE-Advanced. LTE-Advanced exhibits backward and forward compatibility with the LTE system. Some of the areas where LTE-Advanced finds its application include mobile cloud computing, driverless cars, virtual and augmented reality, and 3D video call [16].

5.2.4 ZigBee

ZigBee protocol depends on low-power (1mW or less power) wireless IEEE802.15.4 (operating in the medium access control (MAC) layer) networks standard. IEEE 802.15.4 facilitates a combination of 27 channels which are non-overlapping: 16 operating in the 2.4GHz and 11 operating in the sub-GHz frequency bands. Three topologies are supported by IEEE 802.15.4, consisting of star, cluster tree, or mesh. It supports features such as low power consumption, low transmission, cheap, characteristics with less time delay, easy development and deployment, provision of powerful security, and reliable data. It finds its applications with requirements of low data transmission rate, long-lasting battery, and security of networking devices. It supports all topologies which include mesh, star, and tree network topologies. The responsibility for the initialization, maintenance, and control of the networks lies with the ZigBee coordinator. Numerous ZigBee routers and a single ZigBee coordinator are involved in the formation of a network. Association with a router or coordinator a device can join a network [17].

5.3 SHIFT TOWARDS GREEN IoT

Green IoT (G-IoT) is considered to be another aspect of IoT for achieving environmental sustainability. There has been a tremendous shift towards G-IoT because of its capabilities of reducing carbon emissions, conservation of natural resources, and supporting energy-efficient strategies. This section lays major emphasis on utilization of the existing IoT technologies towards the achievement of a greener environmental system. The process of achieving sustainability is associated with certain challenges and some major requirements [18].

5.3.1 Requirements and Challenges to Green IoT

IoT has gone through numerous infrastructural changes since its inception and the current model; that is, G-IoT has been proposed to achieve low power and energy consumption. This section gives a brief about the requirements of various IoT devices for implementing G-IoT. Further, the implementation is associated with certain challenges which hinder the process and are henceforth discussed as follows:

1. Requirements of green IoT – IoT was established with the aim of connecting a huge number of devices. There is a paradigm shift towards green IoT (G-IoT) because of the rising concern of excessive power consumption by IoT systems/technologies and to ensure environmental sustainability for IoT systems. G-IoT focuses on two major facets:

- Development of energy-efficient computing devices (which is also referred to as green designing), networking architecture, and communication protocols.
- Ensuring the reduction in carbon emissions, pollution, and other environmental damage caused due to IoT technologies, and catering to the industrial demands while ensuring energy efficiency.

There are various technologies for enabling G-IoT including WSNs, energy harvesting devices, RFID, cellular networks, big data analysis, machine-to-machine communication, and cloud computing. The prime focus of G-IoT is towards the following:

- *Green manufacturing* – Production of electronic devices and electronic components/subsystems with minimal impact on the environment while focusing on increasing the recycling rate of the finished products.
- *Green utilization* –Minimizing the power consumption by technologies and other electronic devices and furthermore ensuring environmental sustainability.
- *Green designing* – Enabling the designing, analysis, and synthesis of green IOT computers, servers, and other related devices which are energy efficient.
- Green disposal: Renovating and reusing old gadgets, and recycling unused electronic devices. The lifecycle of G-IoT is shown in Figure 5.3.

There are five major principles that have been analysed and proposed that can be utilized in achieving G-IoT and reduction of carbon footprints. The principles are defined as follows:

- *Selective sensing* – Collecting only the data that is of importance and is required in a particular situation. Elimination of additional data sensing is highly energy efficient.
- *Reduction in network size* – For low energy consumption, the size of the network can be reduced by applying perceptive routing mechanisms and by placing the nodes efficiently.
- *Hybrid architecture* – Utilization of passive and active sensors for various activities in an IoT network system can result in low energy consumption.
- *Intelligent trade-offs* – An optimal balance needs to be maintained between prioritizing costs and energy efficiency using communication techniques like compressive sensing and data fusion.
- *Policy-making* – Productive and efficient policies can have a considerable amount of impact on reduction in energy consumption at smart buildings.

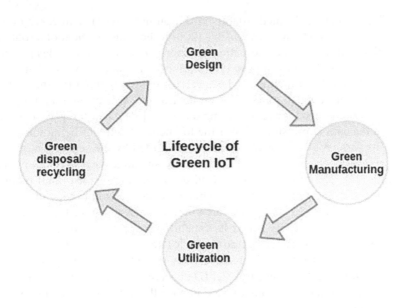

FIGURE 5.3   Lifecycle of green IoT.

2. *Challenges to green IoT* – There have been rigorous ongoing efforts in achieving sustainability and energy-efficient technology, but G-IoT is still struggling in its initial stages due to multiple challenges. The shift to green IoT poses a serious challenge and creates a bottleneck to the computing and efficiency needs. The underlying challenges include the following:

- Performance management after the integration of G-IoT models within the existing IoT architecture.
- Focusing on green design for applications to minimize the environmental impact.
- Reliability of G-IoT after integrating energy consumption models.
- Energy efficiency of both the devices and the protocols used in communication.
- Tackling the increased complexity of the G-IoT infrastructure.
- Compromising between efficient spectrum management and dynamic spectrum sensing.
- Green solutions to reduce power consumption by the middleware layer.
- Efficient security mechanisms such as encryption and control commands.

Reliability is also amongst one of the major challenges to G-IoT and is vital for the efficiency of IoT devices in enabling [19] sustainability. Unreliable sensors, processors, and transmitters can produce false reports of recorded data, increased time for data collection, and loss of data. There have been different routing protocols being developed to establish an energy-efficient

IoT architecture. Pruned Adaptive IoT Routing (PAIR) is an energy efficient protocol which is responsible [20] for the establishment of a routing
path by taking into consideration the energy reserve of the nodes present
in the system for transmitting information to sink nodes. An implementation of an utility function has been carried out for aggregating the cost of
routing for nodes that are involved for transmission of data, and a pric-
ing model is used for representing the same [21]. Data integrity ensures
that the data is transmitted over the IoT network without being modified
in its path. While forwarding the data recorded by the sensors, it can be
modified or the values can be changed by any attacker present along the
path [22]. The modified values lead to production of false final reports
that can cause security threats. This also leads to improper implementation of strategies and procedures opted for ensuring sustainability. A
major concern with G-IoT is its capability to provide the same performance in data integrity as traditional IoT technologies. G-IoT technologies such as RFID have increasingly shown lack in reliability since they
fail to provide data integrity – RFID tags are not enabled with high-level
intelligence and if left unattended expose the data to attacks making it
vulnerable [23].

3. *Green in IoT vs. green by IoT* – Green in IoT are initiatives aimed at reducing the negative environmental impact of IoT, posing an energy-efficient
   green IoT network, whereas green by IoT are initiatives for making a positive environmental impact through IoT implementations. Both the initiatives are essential for reducing the detrimental impact on the environment
   and achieving sustainability. Green in IoT, green computing (also referred
   to as green IT), can be described as the effective study, research, and implementation of environmentally sustainable computing. Energy-efficient IoT
   models have been described as follows:

   - *IoT system model* – In the proposed model, embedded servers are
     connected to devices such as sensors and home appliances. To enable
     a virtual environment for objects, it owns RESTful internet facilities
     for communication with the cloud server. For service lookup, the
     transferring of the virtual objects to server application takes place.
     Application server interface creates a platform to ensure commu-
     nication between the server and client. The cloud server ensures
     any new service implemented, to be tested within the application
     repository before deploying [24,25]. The system model is shown in
     Figure 5.4.

IoT system is composed of sensors equipped with physical devices and IP
addresses. Lesser capable low-power sensors with IP addresses are clustered as relay nodes, whereas better connected and more capable devices
are clustered as sink nodes. Production of the data takes place at the relay
node and transmitted to the sink node. An embedded web server is tasked
with scheduling the physical and sensor devices. IoT systems consist of
devices that are not in action and thus act only upon request. Scheduling

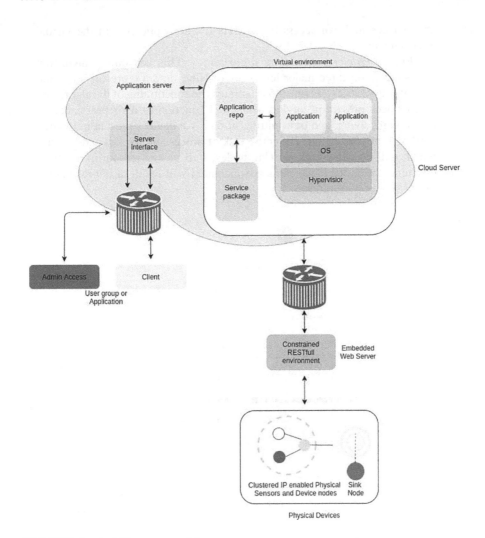

FIGURE 5.4   An IoT system model.

enables energy-efficient devices with the energy consumed directly proportional to the device utilization.

Cloud provides virtualization of the physical objects through a virtual environment in the cloud. Application server is equipped with the ability to establish communication with the client via an interface. Server acts as a registry as it keeps a record of the devices and services in an IoT network. Application repository is responsible for conducting a capability and feature test of the application, and searches defective codes within the service package. User application is the application of the client side. Admin can directly perform any modifications directly and monitor the performance of the system. The client can send request(s) to the application server through an interface and can access the objects of the application in the virtual environment.

- *Energy-efficient scheduling algorithm* – This scheduling algorithm operates on three major levels comprising on-duty, pre-off duty, and off- duty [26,27]. Figure 5.5 illustrates the functioning of the algorithm. The devices present in on-duty state will function to their best capacity. Sensing, receiving, and transmitting of data via devices present in the network will be carried out. The entire task of processing sensors and devices, which will be either sink or relay nodes, will be carried out in a virtual environment on the cloud. This advancement will result in improved data processing opportunities.

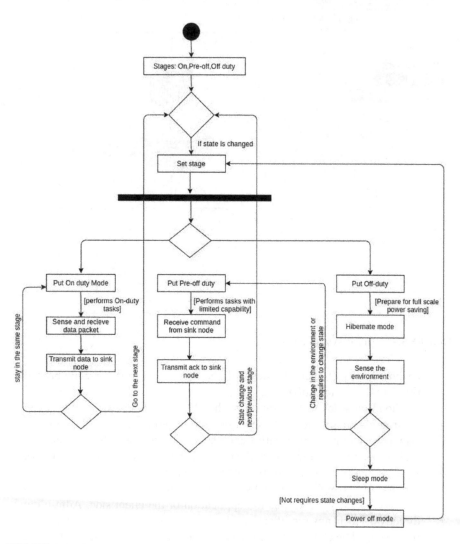

FIGURE 5.5   Stages in the energy efficient algorithm.

Pre-off duty is the bidirectional stage wherein, devices are only involved in receiving and transmitting the data from the sink. A new request sent by the sink node will cause the pre-off stage to change into on duty. While any command sent by the sink node will set the pre-off duty to the associated mode. Off-duty mode is primarily responsible for holding the three states for saving energy in various situations and ensuring an energy-efficient network. The performance evaluation of the three stages is shown in Figure 5.6. The power consumption in on-duty stage is higher compared to the other two stages due to increased task load.

- *Novel development scheme* – This is an optimization model for the development of green IoT. It establishes a system framework for the arrangement of elements in an IoT network. Migration of traffic from sensing to relay node is done by ensuring direct communication between relay nodes and no communication amongst sensing nodes [28]. Depending on the system framework, a model of green IoT has been developed taking into consideration energy consumption constraints. The maximum energy utilization that occurs in IoT is for establishing communication between data/message, as the energy consumption in both sensing of data and its processing is much less compared to transmission. The Friis free space model depicts the energy consumption relation as follows:

$$E_{tx} = \left(E_{elec} + \varepsilon_0 d^2\right) \cdot L \tag{5.2}$$

$$E_{rx} = E_{elec} \cdot L \tag{5.3}$$

where E_{tx} and E_{rx} represent the node energy consumption for transmitting and receiving data, E_{elec} represents the radio electronics energy consumption, $\varepsilon_0, \varepsilon_1$, and ε_2 denote the transmit amplifier of the node, sensing node,

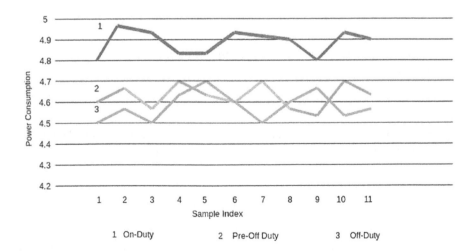

FIGURE 5.6   Power consumption (in Joules) in three stages.

and relay node, respectively, d_{ij} is the distance between node i and node j, and data length is denoted by L.

The energy consumed by each node per unit time is given by the following equations:

$$e_i = \sum_{j \in R} c_{ij} \cdot F_{ij} \cdot \left(E^s_{elec} + 1 \cdot d^2_{ij}\right) \forall i \in S \qquad (5.4)$$

$$e_j = \sum_{i \in S \cup R} c_{ij} \cdot F_{ij} \cdot E^R_{elec} + \sum_{i \in B \cup R} c_{ji} \cdot F_{ji} \cdot \left(E^R_{elec} + 2 \cdot d^2_{ji}\right) \forall j \in R \qquad (5.5)$$

$$e_k = \sum_{j \in R} c_{jk} \cdot F_{jk} \cdot E^B_{elec} \quad \forall k \in B \qquad (5.6)$$

where e_i, e_j, and e_k define the energy consumption of sensing node, relay node, and base station, respectively, and E^s_{elec}, E^R_{elec}, and E^B_{elec} denote the energy consumed by the radio electronics of the sensing node, relay node, and base station, respectively [29,30].

In link flow balance base stations are connected wired connections, thus having a higher bandwidth. Relay nodes are connected through wireless connections satisfying the following constraint:

$$c_{ij} \cdot F_{ij} + c_{ji} \cdot F_{ji} \leq F_{max} \forall i, j \in R \qquad (5.7)$$

where F_{ij} is the data rate from node i to node j and F_{max} the maximum data rate of a link.

The wireless links at each sensing node and base station need to meet the following constraint:

$$c_{ij} \cdot F_{ij} \leq F_{max} \forall i \in S, j \in R \text{ or} \forall i \in R, j \in B \qquad (5.8)$$

During system budget, the base stations and node are costly; hence, the deployment of various IoT devices must satisfy the following system budget constraint:

$$0 < C_s \cdot 1 + C_R \cdot m < W_0 \qquad (5.9)$$

where W_0 is the system budget, and C and C_R depict the cost of sensing and relay node, respectively.

The optimization model aims at reducing the energy consumption by solving the abovementioned constraints taken into consideration as follows:

$$\text{Min } \sum e_i + \sum e_j + \sum e_k \qquad (5.10)$$

$$i \in S \, j \in R \, K \in B$$

A minimal energy consumption algorithm (MECA) has been proposed which operates and depends on the clustering principle and the Steiner tree algorithm to solve the optimization problem [31]. The proposed algorithm is majorly responsible for deployment of green IoT (Liang, 2103).

Algorithm 1 (Source: [30]) MECA

Input: S, R, B, $R \geq r > 0$
Output:
Minimal Energy Consumption min (e)

```
1: Apply K-means clustering algorithm to obtain a single cover
set S1 ⊆ S, choose the closest relay i ∈ R to replace the j ∈
S1 forming the set R1.
2: for i ∈ R, j ∈ R ∪ B, i ≠ j do
3: Calculate the distance d_ij between i and j;
4: if d_ij ≤ R then
5: Add the node i and j to a candidate set RN for placement,
set cij = 1 in G;
6: end if
7: end for
8: Assign edge weight for G in terms of (4), (5) and (6) on
each edge;
9: Apply a well-known Steiner Tree algorithm to compute a
minimal energy consumption Steiner tree GT of G = (S ∪ RN ∪
B, A) spanning the node set B ∪ R1.
10: for each edge in GT do
11: Sum the total weight on each edge, denoted as min (e);
12: end for
13: return min (e);
```

- *Green by IoT* – Green by IoT focuses on the establishment of green computing strategies to meet the rising demands of infrastructure and resources. Urbanization is the major contributing factor to greenhouse gas emissions and energy consumption. IoT aims at transforming these urban cities into "smart cities," with capabilities of effective utilization of information technology for responding to challenges, improving the quality of life, and achieving sustainability goals [32]. The IoT technology is known to establish the correlation and ensure effective management of water, transportation, and energy. Collection of precise, accurate data and analytics are the major contributing factor that aids IoT in handling environmental issues. The data provides us real-time information being actional that regulates wise decision-making, energy efficiency, and effective allocation of resources. The following are some of the IoT technologies described that are used for achieving sustainability:

- Sensor networks and cloud software are responsible for the reduction of economic and environmental impact by an increase in accountability and transparency.
- Installation of sensors while construction ensures better management of temperature and proper ventilation, thereby maintaining energy efficiency and reduction in carbon footprints.
- Environment sensors are equipped with providing real-time data of the system that helps in understanding and solving environmental impacts. These sensors are cheaper and smaller in size, and can be installed at various points across the city. These sensors have been enabled by mobile IoT technology, which is known for providing robust connectivity. These sensors are useful in measuring any parameters including air and water quality, smoke, pollution, weather, and disaster management like flood sensors.
- Smart grids can be instrumental in reducing energy consumption. Reports suggest that smart grids have the ability to save about 2Gt (Gross tonnage) of emissions. This approach provides energy efficiency, precise real-time data. Smart grids come with a huge advantage in terms of energy generation and transmission, providing end users with more control and transparency in their energy usage.
- Installation of sensors [33] in water sources/channels provides real-time information on the consumption of water, its availability, pollution level, quality, biological oxygen demand, and other related water parameters.
- Embedded sensors in highways result in information providing data about fluctuating traffic patterns, thereby enabling more efficient traffic management, and reduction in carbon footprint and greenhouse gases.

5.4   IoT APPLICATIONS

IoT-based systems and models have been implemented in achieving smart cities, smart water management, pollution mitigation, smart medical and healthcare, environmental protection, and smart transportation, amongst others. The application of IoT has shown promising results in both the form of being instrumental in saving resources and funds while also developing newer energy-efficient models. Some of the ground-breaking areas that IoT has been applied in are mentioned in Figure 5.7.

5.4.1   SMART CITIES

Smart sustainable cities are the by-products of the interlinking of the advancements in environmental sustainability, ICT, and urbanization. It is an inventive approach that incorporates IoTs, sensor technology, and ICTs to achieve an improved lifestyle, and competency in urban progression and services. The deployment of sensors is utilized for collecting real-time information and serves as an important unit for

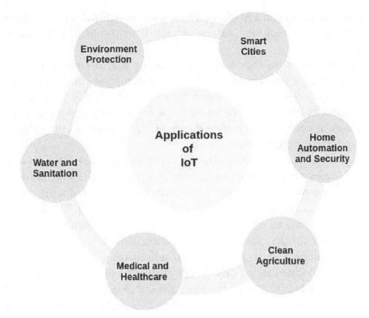

FIGURE 5.7   Applications of IoT.

processing data. Data mining is used for analysing and processing the data recorded by the sensors. This data is further deployed for automation, building models, and enabling decision-making for urban operations, strategies, and procedures for achieving environmental sustainability [34].

Various applications of IoT technologies used for implementing several aspects of smart cities are described as follows:

1. Noise monitoring in such cities can be achieved by measuring and collecting data for noise production at any given time at a particular location by sensors. Noise data collected by sensors is in terms of sound pressure level (SPL) further converted into decibel. Further, this can be supported by constructing a space–time graph for noise pollution. This facility can be further extended in achieving public security, by interpretation and analysis using noise detection algorithms that can determine, such as, the sound of crashing glass [35]. SPL is calculated using in the following equation:

$$SPL = 20\log_{10}\left(P/P_{ref}\right)dB \qquad (5.11)$$

where P is the sound measured and P_{ref} the sound pressure detected by the human ear.

2. Monitoring traffic congestion is also a service provided by smart cities. Deployment of CCTV cameras in traffic monitoring systems already exists in various cities, enabling communication with low power consumption while providing a deeper source of information. GPS installations on

vehicles, and acoustic and air quality sensors combined are used for traffic monitoring. The recorded data is of utmost importance to the managing organizations.

3. Smart parking is another service enabled by IoT in smart cities. This is based primarily on sensors deployed in parking lots and smart displays for guiding drivers to the best parking path. This service provides numerous benefits such as accelerating the time for locating a particular parking slot, thereby reduction in carbon monoxide emission from the vehicles and reduced traffic congestion.

4. Storage of waste and mounted landfills are a major concern for smart cities. Technologies such as smart waste bins detect the load levels, allowing the optimization of the truck path of the collector, further reducing the expenditure of waste collection and improved recycling quality. The IoT connects the smart waste bins, to a central control system, consisting of an optimization software for the evaluation of the data recorded.

5. Smart street light system is aimed to reduce the power consumption by street lights located in the city. This system also enables automatic ON or OFF of the lights by sensing the movement of objects. It uses LED bulbs as the source of light, which consume less power and are triggered by multi-sensors. Resistance of devices equipped with IR LED lights decreases in the presence of light and increases in dark. IR sensor senses/detects and captures the signal from a person and vehicle on the road, and the signal transmitted from the sensor helps in switching ON the street light [36]. Figure 5.8 defines the infrastructure of the system.

6. Boosting the productivity of the public workers while reducing the energy consumption by monitoring public buildings such as colleges, libraries, and administrative offices is carried out by means of installed WSNs that control the temperature, ambient lighting, etc.

7. Heritage preservation is also one of the services provided by smart cities enabled by IoT technologies. There are appropriate sensors installed in the buildings for monitoring building stress deformation and vibration sensors, atmospheric agents, etc. The result of these sensors provides a distributed database of buildings and can be used for the maintenance of the building.

5.4.2 HOME AUTOMATION AND SMART SECURITY

Home automation systems are seeing a rapid growth in popularity, providing ease of living, comfort, and security to the owners. Most home automation systems reduce human labour with respect to day-to-day activities and are hence especially useful in case of elderly or disabled owners [37]. The management and monitoring of the home automation system can be facilitated by various devices such as PCs, laptops, desktops, and smartphones, which is a huge advantage of this system. The home automation system is equipped with different sets of sensors enabling data aggregation pertaining to residents and services consumption at various households. The data recorded by the sensors is analysed and interpreted for identifying the actions required by the residents.

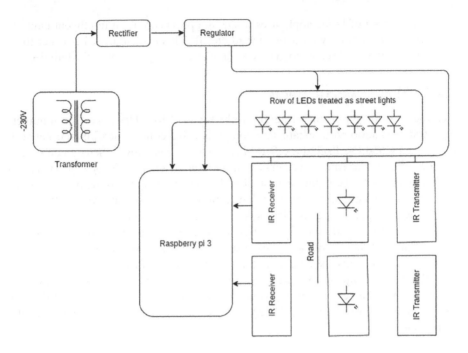

FIGURE 5.8   The process of smart street light system.

1. *Smart security system* – Passive infrared sensors (PIR) are used for detecting the movements and actions of human beings. The building entrance is equipped with these sensors which behave as motion detectors. Sensors are instituted at all entrances but are controlled by a single microcontroller. While detecting the motion, a signal is sent as an input trigger for the microcontroller. This dial has a voice call (on a pre-installed number) warning the owner of the presence of an unknown person. This can further be connected to the alarm system or calling the authorities in the police department. The owner can remotely control the lights or the alarms, but by default, the module is programmed to switch the alarm and lights off after a specified duration.

2. *Smart home automation system* – Various wireless home automation systems have been under research recently based on the ZigBee module. RF ZigBee modules are the basis of wireless networking as these modules are energy-efficient and cost-effective. This system comprises three major modules: handheld microphone module, central controller module, and appliance controller module. The central controller module is PC based, and the handheld microphone module implements ZigBee protocol [38]. Voice recognition software is also introduced as a layer of security using Microsoft API. The basic operations include controlling the energy management systems and household appliances such as electronic lamps, ventilation, and air conditioning (HVAC) while providing the user unrestricted

monitoring of home appliances usage and provision of an intelligent environment for energy reduction based on IoT. This even allows the owner to remotely provide entry to guests without even being present in the building.

5.4.3 MEDICAL AND HEALTHCARE

Healthcare is an important paradigm in the focus of IoT. There have been numerous strategies adopted to establish a comprehensive communication and network between IoT and the healthcare field. IoT devices consisting of sensors and other components such as trans-receivers and microcontrollers are responsible for aggregation, analysis, and communication of real-time healthcare and medical information onto the cloud, thereby ensuring collection, storage, and analysis of this data. IoT-based healthcare and medical system is capable of monitoring the physical parameters of hospital and client patients, which results in reduction in cost and enhancement of quality of care. This system combines mobile computation, medical sensors, and network communication technology. GPRS, ZigBee, Bluetooth, and WLAN are various wireless technologies used in the healthcare system. There has been a recent development of comfortable wearable medical devices by the integration of ECG, SpO2 sensors, and accelerometer [39] utilized for the following:

1. *Diabetes* – Sensing of non-invasive glucose on a real-time basis. Sensors injected into patients are linked through IPv6 connectivity to suitable medical and healthcare centres. The device consists of a blood glucose detector, a smart cellular device or PC, and a processor in the background. For monitoring the blood glucose level, a medical accretion detector is used.
2. *Regulation of body temperature* – To monitor the fluctuation in body temperature, a TelosBmote (WSN) temperature sensor is implanted in the body and the received report is then analysed for providing necessary prescription. The RFID and body temperature monitoring modules are the core components responsible for recording of temperature and its transmission.
3. *Monitoring blood pressure* – IoT-based blood pressure (BP) regulating model has two main components – a BP meter/monitor device and an NFC-accredited smartphone. IoT devices aim at enabling and monitoring the communication between medical post, and medical and healthcare centres. A location intelligent terminal is assigned the collection and transmission of the BP data over the IoT network.
4. *Oxygen saturation* – Saturation of oxygen in blood can be measured with a pulse oximetry and a non-invasive continuous monitoring system. Integrated pulse oximetry is advantageous for IoT-based healthcare and medical applications. A wearable pulse oximeter device for health regulation based on the WSN can be integrated to the IoT network.
5. *Electrocardiogram (ECG) detection* – ECG is defined as the electrical action of the heart which can be registered by electrocardiography. This is done by measuring the heart rate for the detection of the rhythm as well as the diagnosis of myocardial ischemia, prolonged QT intervals, and

arrhythmias. A search automation method is integrated into the system for detecting the peculiar data such that the identification of cardiac function can be carried out on a real-time basis.

6. *Wheelchair management* –This approach provides methods for controlling the chair vibration and detection of the wheelchair status. This IoT-based wheelchair is equipped with technology for monitoring and collecting the appropriate data of the clients surrounding and interlinking the collected data with the GPS. Android application is in connection with the wheel-chair by interfacing the Wi-Fi module with the Arduino microcontroller (IC ATMEGA328). IC L293D motor driver circuitry is used for simulating the movement in the wheelchair. Any obstacle is detected by IR sensors present in all directions. Various sensors [40] including pulse detecting and temperature sensors are deployed in health monitoring systems [41]. Figure 5.9 displays the system architecture of wheelchair system.

7. *Medication management* – IoT-based medical and healthcare system addresses the issue of medication management with an e-Health architecture. The medication control system is based on RFID tags for the IoT network. The packaging method adopted for medicine boxes includes a prototype system of the I2Pack and the iMedBox providing system confirmation by field trials. This method also incorporates controlled sealing based on delamination materials controlled by wireless communications.

5.4.4 SMART AGRICULTURE

IoT and automation technology have been adopted for enabling smart agriculture [43], further boosting productivity and efficiency in this labour-intensive field. The major focus of smart agriculture is to monitor the climatic and environmental

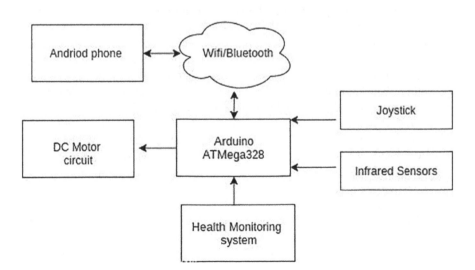

FIGURE 5.9 System architecture of wheelchair system.

changes because these factors affect the crops and plants the most. Smart agriculture equipped with sensors provides numerous advantages such as precise analysis of nutrients and minerals dearth, lower power and energy consumption automation, water and pollution management, accurate agricultural data collection, storage and its analysis, optimized energy resources, online crop monitoring, and real-time information about varying weather patterns and crop changes.

Temperature, pressure, humidity, moisture, and water level sensors are used for gathering real-time information related to soil fertility, pest, weed and insect detection, moisture, temperature etc. Unmanned aerial vehicles have been adopted for crop surveillance and activities such as weeding, spraying, and cutting of crops. The farm conditions are monitored using WSNs, and microcontrollers are used for controlling and automating the cultivation process. Installation of wireless cameras is used for viewing locally the farm condition. Farmers are kept updated and informed through smart phones, which also enables communication amongst different farmers, scientists, and labs. The system of smart agriculture is implemented through various methodologies. This system comprises the following sections [42]:

1. GPS-established vehicles which are controlled remotely by a central computer/PC. It can also be automated to ensure its navigation within the entire crop field by utilizing the field coordinates provided by the GPS module. This vehicle is equipped with a microcontroller, which is in turn connected to a GPS module, power supply, moisture, humidity, and obstacle and temperature sensor. Various tasks are performed such as spraying pesticides and fertilizers, scaring fowls, cutting crops and plants, and monitoring environmental factors. The soil data is collected by soil moisture sensors. The data recorded by the sensors are forwarded to Raspberry Pi, the microcontroller. The obstacle sensor helps in detecting any obstacle approaching the vehicle head-on, to prevent collision by changing directions.

2. Enforcement of smart warehouse management. There is a central AVR controller which is connected to sensors such as temperature sensor, motion detector sensor, humidity sensors, heater, cooling fan, alarm, and water pump. The humidity and temperature sensors are utilized for detecting humidity, and if the level of humidity crosses a threshold value, the cooling fan is switched ON automatically until the humidity reaches the threshold value. In the case where humidity is below threshold value, the heater is switched ON to increase the temperature. These operations are remotely observed and managed through a connected smart device and the operations will be performed by ZigBee modules interfaced with sensors and a microcontroller.

3. The data recorded by the sensors in the two sections are then forwarded to cloud which further delivers the data to a mobile app. The farmer can interact with the mobile app and obtain all data pertaining to the crop field and the warehouse. The app provides multiple options through which the farmer can control and monitor the farms and warehouse. The prevention of theft

in the warehouse is ensured by the buzzer sound which is automatically made by the app, allowing the farmers to take necessary steps to control theft.

5.4.5 WATER AND SANITATION

Water leakage detection, water quality in different water bodies, and water meter reading are some of the smart water applications. IoT has enabled water monitoring and management to detect the quality of water and various other water-related parameters to reduce water contamination. The boost in IoT-based smart water management has enabled solving various water-related issues with the help of IoT systems equipped with WSNs, transmitters, and microcontrollers. Water leakage in pipes is detected using various IoT equipped devices, and the information recorded is made available on the cloud. The water quality is measured and monitored in real time using various sensors, and the information recorded is made available on the cloud. The related water quality and parameter information is utilized by water management organizations for the preservation of quality of water. Sensors are used for recording the various water-related parameters such as water level, turbidity, temperature, CO_2, pH, and alkalinity. The functions of the water sensors are described as follows:

1. *pH sensor* – The pH range can vary from acidic, neutral to alkaline. The water is reported to be acidic if the pH value recorded is less than 7 and basic for pH value larger than 7. pH value 7 is considered to be a neutral or balanced state. The value of pH ranges from 0 to 14.
2. *CO_2 sensors* – This sensor is used for measuring the carbon dioxide concentration in water. SKU: SEN0219, an analog infrared sensor, is used in the sensor for measuring the CO_2 content. CO_2 is measured in parts per million (ppm).
3. *Turbidity sensor* – SKU: SEN0189 is the turbidity sensor used for detecting the turbidity level of water. The turbidity sensor detects the presence of suspended particles in water by measurement of analogue/digital signal output modes, and the selection of the modes is carried out by the microcontroller unit (MCU).The turbidity sensor is operable on 5 V DC voltage and 40mA (maximum) current.
4. *Salt sensor* – It is used to calculate the alkalinity of the sewage water, and the data recorded is made available across the web browser with the help of microcontroller. It comprises two rods: measuring and reference rods. The reference rod is provided with voltage, and current is conducted to the measuring rod. Salt concentration in the water is directly proportional to the voltage at the measuring rod.
5. *Water level sensor* – It is most widely used for water level detection, water leakage, and rainfall. It is mainly composed of three components: 1MΩ resistor, numerous lines of bare conducting wires, and an electronic brick connector. The 1MΩ resistor pulls up the sensor value until a drop of water shorts the sensor trace to the grounded trace. Exposed parallel wires can

accurately calculate the size of the water droplet consuming minimal power [44].

6. *Temperature sensor* – The output voltage of the sensor is in linear proportion to the temperature conditions. The LM35 sensor is responsible for Kelvin to Celsius conversion of the resulting temperature. It measures both heat and cold temperatures.

7. A basic smart water monitoring system utilizes the salt, turbidity, and pH sensors and transmits the recorded water quality data to the microcontroller. The microcontroller computes different water parameters, and the result is displayed through ESP8266 Wi-Fi module. The system design for the same is shown in Figure 5.10 [45].

8. *Automated meter reading (AMR)* – Water meters are equipped with this technology. Automatic collection of data concerned with water consumption, diagnosis, and status data from water meters is the objective of AMR. The collected data is transferred to a central database for billing, troubleshooting, and analysis. Network technologies comprising GSM modem, Wi-Fi, and power line communication have been adopted by AWR.

5.4.6 ENVIRONMENT PROTECTION

Environment monitoring has garnered more attention in recent years with the growing distress caused by climate change. IoT is capable of monitoring both aquatic and atmospheric environments such as wind, sound, and soil. The atmosphere and various environmental resources get contaminated by various types of pollutants which have a detrimental effect on both the climate and the environment in general [46]. The IoT system enables the recording of real-time data of the concentration of the various pollutants using various sensors. For monitoring air pollution, real-time information about various air pollutants such as carbon dioxide(CO_2), carbon monoxide(CO), nitrogen dioxide(NO_2), ultraviolet radiations, and smoke and dust particles, air pressure, and temperature are recorded using various sensors. The air sensors used are as follows:

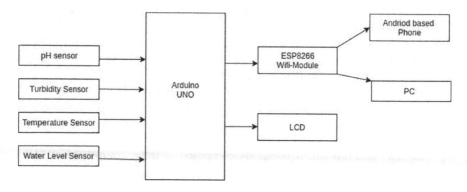

FIGURE 5.10   A system designed for a water monitoring system.

1. *CO and NO₂ sensors* – These sensors are used for detecting the amount of carbon monoxide (CO) present in the atmosphere, and the information is provided to the microcontroller. MICS-5525 and MICS-2710 are examples of CO and NO_2 sensors, respectively.
2. *Pressure and temperature sensors* – These sensors are used for detecting the air temperature and pressure. BMP085 is an example for these sensors.
3. *UV radiation sensor* – UV sensors display an analog signal as the output of the amount of UV light. UVI-01 is a UV sensor.
4. *General air quality sensors* – These sensors are used for measuring the quality of air and also for determining whether it is fit for breathing. TGS 2600 is one such sensor.

Water pollution monitoring is achieved by measuring various water parameters such as alkalinity, pH, turbidity, biological oxygen demand (BOD), carbon dioxide (CO_2), ammonia, and nitrites. The model collects real-time data of the parameters mentioned above and classifies the water quality and portability using machine learning algorithms. SeWatch is a sewage and wastewater wireless monitoring system which detects the sewer overflow in the locality. The information regarding spills and overflowing manholes is reported by the water level sensors to an application. Light radiations from satellites can be used for detecting the water pollution level. It utilizes the pollutant wavelength for identifying the type of pollutant.

The National Institute of Environmental Health Sciences initiated the wearable radio frequency identifier (RFID) [47] sensor project, aimed at developing sensors that work by combining RFID tracking along with sharp gas-detecting capabilities and further detect toxic pollutants in the atmosphere. The result of the sensors can be used to determine the air quality.

The rising pollution also has an impact on the climate, thereby leading to climate changes. Remote sensing is used for disaster management. Early warning systems are established with warning lines created sensors distributed in disaster prone areas. Sensors like unmanned aerial vehicles such as drones and geo-referenced video can be deployed in such region. The system can release warnings and alert the authorities ensuring public security. Geographic Information Systems (GIS) [48] finds its application in analysing the topography of a catchment area and uses various models and architecture for comparing the peak discharge against the minimum peak discharge. There exist various earthquake warning systems in many countries to alert the authorities about the intensity of the earthquake. A Chilean earthquake early warning system comprises an earthquake detector which is installed on an Arduino board. A computer is connected to the board. Instead of an alert system, it has been advanced for sending a tweet.

5.5 CASE STUDY: SANTANDER CITY

This section discusses the IoT architecture and experimentation centre that is currently deployed in Santander city. Project Santander is an experimental test facility under the EU for research and evaluation of large-scale architecture, key enabling technologies, and services and applications for the IoT in the context of a smart city.

The aim of this facility is to implement the findings of the research community on key IoT technologies in a large-scale experiment evaluating it under real-world conditions [49]. A city-wide implementation of an experimental facility has special significance for IoT research for three main reasons:

1. The technologies that are implemented in Santander as part of the smart city infrastructure and the city-wide daily user experience generated with its use [50].
2. The heterogeneity of the devices and the number of users involved in the experiment.
3. The problems generated in large-scale implementation in such ecosystems like smart cities are invaluable to research advancements in the field of IoT.

As depicted in Figure 5.11, the city-wide test implementation is realized by a three-tiered architecture: perception tier, gateway (middleware) tier, and server tier.

The perception layer consists of the devices installed around the city in places such as public parks, street lights, and parking areas. Aimed at maximizing the applications of the deployed devices, the perception layer has a wide range of device types such as smartphones, RFID tags, and a wide variety of WSN platforms. The middleware layer connects the perception tier with the core architecture and the internet. The devices in the middleware layer are programmable, in order to incorporate different solutions and experimentation, while not having to reconfigure the integration with the network layer. The devices in the middleware layer typically have more computational power with larger memories, and continuous power input.

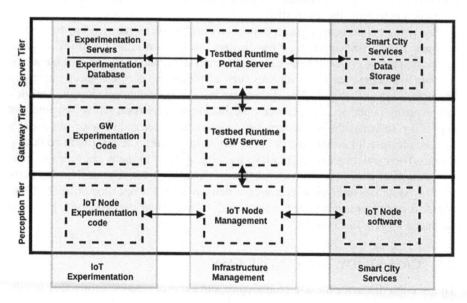

FIGURE 5.11   Three-tiered node and plane architecture.

The network layer is tasked with both processing and storing the data collected city-wide [51].

There are three major areas of IoT architecture that have been deployed in Santander city: infrastructure management, IoT experimentation, and smart city services. The functioning and complete operation of the infrastructure is ensured by APIs and various software peripherals, which are contained by the infrastructure management. This area supports features such as node/GW registration and composition, user authentication, IoT node reservation, monitoring and measuring of data, data aggregation, and its security. The area of IoT experimentation supports functions such as deployment of experimentation code, abstraction of the experiment output data, and managed and monitored experiment. Regular inflow of data to smart cities for enabling energy efficient services is ensured by the software peripherals and APIs present at all tiers and composed by the area of smart city.

First of its kind IoT services have been installed in Santander with the idea of research and development in mind. Some of the facilities that have been made available by the introduction of IoT are as follows:

1. *Outdoor parking management* – The main feature of the parking management system is the real-time display of the free parking spots around the city. Ferromagnetic wireless sensors have been installed in the limited parking spaces available in Santander. The information is collected and subsequently sent to the middleware from where it is transferred to the user applications and to displays on city junctions informing the citizens of the free spots around the city.

2. *Garden monitoring and precision irrigation* – Garden monitoring and irrigation provides real-time information of the status of the parks to the technicians and gardening authorities, allowing them to assess the conditions remotely. Sensors have been installed both above ground (for monitoring atmospheric conditions) and underground (for measuring parameters like soil moisture) in two parks in Santander. Alerts are set to notify the garden authorities when aberrant conditions are sensed.

3. *Environment monitoring* – A considerable number of environment monitoring systems are deployed in Santander. Nodes of air pollution and noise WSNs have been deployed at various street lights around the city. To expand the node network and coverage of the city, devices have also been installed in public transport and vehicles belonging to the government.

4. *Participatory sensing* – This service requires the users permission for their phone to be used as a sensing device to collect information such as noise and temperature. The collected information is then processed and collected in the SmartSantander platform providing useful information for the areas where sensors haven't been deployed. This application also allows users to get alerts for events (road congestion, cultural events, protests, accidents, etc.) that are going on around the city.

5.6 FUTURE ADVANCEMENTS

G-IoT, with respect to research, is still in its infant stages and hence shows significant potential as a future prospect. G-IoT has numerous aspects to be focused upon with respect to achieving environmental sustainability. The future prospects in G-IoT introduce new technologies replacing the existing ones with less power consumption and high performance. The future technologies assist application by acquiring accurate real-time data and providing its control to the user for further development. Some of the future research directions affecting G-IoT are given as follows:

1. *SNaaS* – Virtualized sensor as a service (SNaaS) provides ease of data management along with the scope for providing complete access and control of the data to the users, developing it into a private IoT security concern caused by G-IoT models.
2. *Sensor cloud* – Sensor cloud is an extension of cloud computing for WSN management, providing efficient integration of internet services, WSN network, and cloud computing. Sensor cloud has uses in numerous applications, especially in systems requiring collection and processing of data from large WSNs. There is further scope for development of protocols in sensor cloud for integration.

These advancements in the field of G-IoT have the potential to considerably impact future architecture designs and research areas in the field of IoT.

5.7 CONCLUSIONS

The IoT has proved to be a revolutionary technology. It has enabled the communication and networking between various devices, through its comprehensive architecture comprising of various layers and the efficient technologies involved with it. IoT supports numerous features but faces the major challenge of increased energy consumption and increased carbon footprint. The technology is not energy-efficient and also has a detrimental impact on the environment hampering sustainability. There has been a paradigm shift towards green IoT(G-IoT) to tackle the issue of energy efficiency. G-IoT has the capability of reducing carbon emissions, conserving natural resources, and supporting energy efficient strategies. The lifecycle of G-IoT majorly focuses on green design, green production, green utilization, and green disposal. There are various hardware and software challenges faced in implementing G-IoT. Green computing strategies to meet the rising demands on infrastructure and resources are being adopted. IoT supports the implementation of G-IoT by the deployment of various sensors and technologies such as embedded sensors, temperature and air sensors, water sensors, and smart grids. IoT-based technologies, models, and systems have been implemented in achieving smart cities, smart water management, pollution mitigation, smart medical and healthcare, environmental protection, and smart transportation amongst other numerous applications. IoT models deployed in these areas to provide real-time precise data for achieving environmental sustainability and effective allocation of resources.

REFERENCES

1. Atzori, L., Iera, A., & Morabito, G. (2010). The Internet of Things: A Survey. Computer Networks, 2787–2805. doi: 10.1016/j.comnet.2010.05.010.
2. Popa, D., Popa, D. D., & Codescu, M.-M. (2017). Reliability for a Green Internet of Things. *Buletinul AGIR*, nr, 45–50.
3. Gubbi, J., Buyya, R., Marusic, S., & Palaniswami, M. (2013). Internet of Things (IoT): A Vision, Architectural Elements, and Future Directions. *Future Generation Computer Systems*, 29(7), 1645–1660. doi: 10.1016/j.future.2013.01.010.
4. Rao, T. V. N., Saheb, S. K., & Reddy, A. J. R. (2017). Design of Architecture for Efficient Integration of Internet of Things and Cloud Computing. *International Journal*, 8, pp. 3–4.
5. Xuyong, H. (2008). *Basic Research of Wireless Sensor Networks and Applications in Power System*. Huazhong University of Science & Technology, Wuhan.
6. Silva, B., Khan, M., & Han, K. (2017). Internet of Things: A Comprehensive Review of Enabling Technologies, Architecture, and Challenges. *IETE Technical Review*, 35, 1–16. doi: 10.1080/02564602.2016.1276416.
7. Lin, J., Yu, W., Zhang, N., Yang, X., Zhang, H., & Zhao, W. (2017). A Survey on Internet of Things: Architecture, Enabling Technologies, Security and Privacy, and Applications. *IEEE Internet of Things Journal*, 4(5), 1125–1142. doi: 10.1109/jiot.2017.2683200.
8. Li, T., Wu, S. S. Chen, S., & Yang, M. C. (2012). Generalized Energy-Efficient Algorithms for the RFID Estimation Problem. *IEEE/ACM Transactions on Networking*, pp. 1978–1990. doi: 10.1109/TNET.2012.2192448.
9. Wang, J., Mei, Z., & Wei, L. F. (2011). Realization of Wireless Communication Card Based on UWB for Industrial Internet of Things. *Advanced Materials Research*, 216, 360–363. doi: 10.4028/www.scientific.net/amr.216.360.
10. Ye, W., Heidemann, J., & Estrin, D. (2002). An Energy-Efficient MAC Protocol for Wireless Sensor Networks, INFOCOM 2002. *Twenty-First Annual Joint Conference of the IEEE Computer and Communications Societies. Proceedings. IEEE*, pp. 1567–1576.
11. Gomez, C., & Paradells, J. (2010). Wireless Home Automation Networks: A Survey of Architectures and Technologies. *Communications Magazine, IEEE*, 48, 92–101. doi: 10.1109/MCOM.2010.5473869.
12. Lin, J., Yu, W., Zhang, N., Yang, X., Zhang, H., & Zhao, W. (2017). A Survey on Internet of Things: Architecture, Enabling Technologies, Security and Privacy, and Applications. *IEEE Internet of Things Journal*, 4(5), 1125–1142. doi: 10.1109/jiot.2017.2683200.
13. Alarcon-Aquino, V., Domínguez-Jiménez, M., & Ohms, C. (2008). Desing and Implementation of a Security Layer for RFID Systems. *Journal of Applied Research and Technology*, 6, 69–82. doi: 10.22201/icat.16656423.2008.6.02.506.
14. Lu, C.-W., Li, S.-C., & Wu, Q. (2011). Interconnecting ZigBee and 6LoWPAN wireless sensor networks for smart grid applications. *Sensing Technology (ICST), 2011 Fifth International Conference*, pp. 267–272.
15. Cerruela, G., Luque Ruiz, I., & Gómez-Nieto, M. (2016). State of the Art, Trends and Future of Bluetooth Low Energy, Near Field Communication and Visible Light Communication in the Development of Smart Cities. *Sensors*, 16, 1968. doi: 10.3390/s16111968.
16. Al-Fuqaha, A., Guizani, M., Mohammadi, M., Aledhari, M., & Ayyash, M. (2015). Internet of Things: A Survey on Enabling Technologies, Protocols, and Applications. *IEEE Communications Surveys & Tutorials*, 17, 2347–2376.

17. Sheng, X., Tang, J., Xiao, X., & Xue, G. (2013). Sensing as a Service: Challenges, Solutions and Future Directions. *Sensors Journal, IEEE*, 13, 3733–3741. doi: 10.1109/ JSEN.2013.2262677.

18. Alsamhi, S., Ma, O., Ansari, S., & Meng, Q. (2018). Greening Internet of Things for Smart Everythings with a Green-Environment Life: A Survey and Future Prospects, 6–8.

19. Chen, J.-X., & Wu, M. (2018). The Application of the Internet of Things in Greenhouse. *International Journal of Computer Trends and Technology*, 58, 62–64. 10.14445/22312803/IJCTT-V58P110.

20. Jiang, D., Zhang, P., Lv, Z., & Song, H. (2016). Energy-Efficient Multiconstraint Routing Algorithm with Load Balancing for Smart City Applications. *IEEE Internet of Things Journal*, 3, 1437–1447.

21. Gapchup, A., Wani, A., Wadghule A., & Jadhav, S. (2017). Emerging Trends of Green IoT for Smart World. *International Journal of Innovative Research in Computer and Communication Engineering*, (5), 2139–2148.

22. Redclift, M. (1992). Sustainable Development and Global Environmental Change Implications of a Changing Agenda. *Global Environmental Change*, 2, 32–42. doi: 10.1016/0959-3780(92)90034-5.

23. Gubbi, J., Buyya, R., Marusic, S., & Palaniswami, M. (2012). Internet of Things (IoT): A Vision, Architectural Elements, and Future Directions. *Future Generation Computer Systems*, 29, 1645–1660. doi: 10.1016/j.future.2013.01.010.

24. Krco, S., Pokric, B., & Carrez, F. (2014). Designing IoT architecture(s): A European perspective. *2014 IEEE World Forum on Internet of Things, WF-IoT 2014*, pp. 79–84. doi: 10.1109/WF-IoT.2014.6803124.

25. Shelby, Z. (2011). Embedded Web Services. Wireless Communications. *IEEE*, 17, 52–57. doi: 10.1109/MWC.2010.5675778.

26. Albers, S. (2010). Energy-Efficient Algorithms. *Communications of the ACM*, 53(5). doi: 10.1145/1735223.1735245.

27. Zhang, J., Iyer, S., Schaumont, P., & Yang, Y. (2012). Simulating power/energy consumption of sensor nodes with flexible hardware in wireless networks. *Annual IEEE Communications Society Conference on Sensor, Mesh and Ad Hoc Communications and Networks workshops*, Vol 1., pp. 112–120. doi: 10.1109/SECON.2012.6275767.

28. Heinzelman, W., Chandrakasan, A., & Balakrishnan, H. (2002). An Application-Specific Protocol Architecture for Wireless Microsensor Networks. *IEEE Transactions on Wireless Communications*, 1(4), 660–670.

29. Amadou, I., Chelius, G., & Valois, F. (2011). Energy-efficient beacon-less protocol for WSN. *2011 IEEE 22nd International Symposium on Personal, Indoor and Mobile Radio Communications*, pp. 990–994. doi: 10.1109/PIMRC.2011.6140118.

30. Abdullah, S. Dr., & Yang, K. (2013). An energy-efficient message scheduling algorithm in Internet of Things environment. *2013 9th International Wireless Communications and Mobile Computing Conference, IWCMC 2013*, pp. 311–316. doi: 10.1109/ IWCMC.2013.6583578.

31. Liang, J.-M., Chen, J.-J., Cheng, H.-H., & Tseng, Y.-C. (2013). An Energy-Efficient Sleep Scheduling with QoS Consideration in 3GPP LTE-Advanced Networks for Internet of Things. *IEEE Journal on Emerging and Selected Topics in Circuits and Systems*, 3, 13–22. doi: 10.1109/JETCAS.2013.2243631.

32. Lloyd, E., & Xue, G. (2007). Relay Node Placement in Wireless Sensor Networks. *IEEE Transactions on Computers*, 56, 134–138. doi: 10.1109/TC.2007.250629.

33. Cuomo, F., Abbagnale, A., & Cipollone, E. (2013). Cross-Layer Network Formation for Energy-Efficient IEEE 802.15.4/ZigBee Wireless Sensor Networks. *Ad Hoc Networks*, 11, 672–686. doi: 10.1016/j.adhoc.2011.11.006.

34. Fernández Áñez, V. (2016). Stakeholders Approach to Smart Cities: A Survey on Smart City Definitions, 157–167. doi: 10.1007/978-3-319-39595-1_16.

35. Silva, W., Alvaro, A., Tomas, G., Afonso, R., Dias, K., & Garcia, V. (2013). Smart cities software architectures: A survey. *Proceedings of the ACM Symposium on Applied Computing*, pp. 1722–1727. doi: 10.1145/2480362.2480688.

36. Leccese, F., Marco, C., & Trinca, D. (2014). A Smart City Application: A Fully Controlled Street Lighting Isle Based on Raspberry-Pi Card, a ZigBee Sensor Network and WiMAX. *Sensors (Basel, Switzerland)*, 14, 24408–24424. doi: 10.3390/s141224408.

37. Bethapudi, P. Dr., Alekhya, M., Reddy, G. K., Geethika A., & Reddy, B. S. (2018). IOT Based Monitoring and Control System for Home Automation. *International Journal of Research*, 5, 4120–4124.

38. Tharaniya, B. S. S., & Soundhari, M. (2015). Intelligent Interface Based Speech Recognition for Home Automation Using Android Application.

39. Nagavelli, R., & Rao, C. (2011). Degree disease possibility (DDP): A mining based statistical measuring approach for disease prediction in health care data mining. *International Conference on Recent Advances and Innovations in Engineering*, ICRAIE 2014. doi: 10.1109/ICRAIE.2014.6909265.

40. Sahoo, P., Mohapatra, S., & Wu, S.-L. (2017). Analyzing Healthcare Big Data with Prediction for Future Health Conditions. *IEEE Access*, 11(2), 1–1. doi: 10.1109/ACCESS.2016.2647619.

41. Xu, B., Xu, L., Cai, H., Xie, C., Hu, J., & Bu, F. (2014). Ubiquitous Data Accessing Method in IoT-Based Information System for Emergency Medical Services. *IEEE Transactions on Industrial Informatics*, 10(2), 1578–1586. doi: 10.1109/TII.2014.2306382.

42. Maksiimovici, M., & Omanovic-Miklicanin, E. (2017). Green internet of things and green nanotechnology role in realizing smart and sustainable agriculture. *VIII International Scientific Agriculture Symposium "AGROSYM 2017"*, Jahorina, Bosnia and Herzegovina.

43. Sushanth, G., & Sujatha, S. (2018). IoT based smart agriculture system. in the Institute of Electrical and Electronic Engineers. doi: 10.1109/WiSPNET.2018.8538702.

44. Sambath, M., Prasant, M., Raghava, N., & Jagadeesh, S. (2019). Iot Based Garden Monitoring System. *Journal of Physics: Conference Series*, 1362, 012069. doi: 10.1088/1742–6596/1362/1/012069.

45. Kamienski, C., Soininen, J.-P., Taumberger, M., Fernandes, S., Toscano, A., Cinotti, T., Maia, R., & Neto, A. (2018). SWAMP: an IoT-based Smart Water Management Platform for Precision Irrigation in Agriculture. doi: 10.1109/GIOTS.2018.8534541.

46. SWAMP: Smart Water Management Platform - Overview and Security Challenges. doi: 10.1109/DSN-W.2018.00024.

47. Bruntland, G. (1987). World Commission on Environment and Development, Our Common Future.

48. Vögler, M., Schleicher, J., Inzinger, C., Dustdar, S., & Ranjan, R. (2016). Migrating Smart City Applications to the Cloud. *IEEE Cloud Computing*, 3, 72–79. doi: 10.1109/MCC.2016.44.

49. Schaffers, H., Komninos, N., Pallot, M., Trousse, B., Nilsson, M., & Oliveira, A. (2011). Smart Cities and the Future Internet: Towards Cooperation Frameworks for Open Innovation. *Future Internet Lecture Notes in Computer Science*, 6656, 431–446. doi: 10.1007/978-3-642-20898-0_31.

50. Vlahogianni, E., Kepaptsoglou, K., Tsetsos, V., & Karlaftis, M. (2015). A Real-Time Parking Prediction System for Smart Cities. *Journal of Intelligent Transportation Systems*, 20, 282–291. doi: 10.1080/15472450.2015.1037955.

51. Nam, T., & Pardo, T. (2011). Conceptualizing a smart city with dimensions of technology, people, and institutions. *ACM International Conference Proceeding Series*, pp. 282–291. doi: 10.1145/2037556.2037602.

Index

Milton Keynes UK
Ingram Content Group UK Ltd.
UKHW040050071024
449327UK00019B/459